A WATCHMAN'S GUIDE TO
PRAYING
GOD'S PROMISES

DICK EASTMAN

PERMISSION TO REPRODUCE

**For information on the ministry of Every Home for Christ,
please visit our website: www.EHC.org.**

A 31-DAY PRAYER GUIDE FOR WATCHMEN ON A "WALL OF PRAYER!"

(Designed for any 24/7 prayer ministry or individual who desires to pray in unity and harmony with other intercessors for the fulfillment of God's promises in the nations.)

The author has chosen to receive no royalties or profit from the sale or distribution of this guide.

CONTENTS

A Call to the Wall

Your Invitation to Join
History's Greatest Prayer Movement!

As you read these words the greatest prayer movement in the history of the Church has begun rising up everywhere. It is Christ-centered and harvest focused. It involves not only powerful prayer but passionate worship. It is a movement of 24/7, day and night prayer and worship over the nations and peoples who are yet to experience the joy of knowing Jesus Christ as Savior.

It is a movement to mobilize "Walls of Prayer" in cities, towns, and regions that consist of all 168 hours in any given week covered continuously with worshiping intercessors who will each take weekly set times (usually one hour each time) for prayer and worship. It is methodical and systematic. It requires leadership and dedication to be sure each Wall is always filled with devoted intercessors. In some settings a Wall of Prayer involves a center or prayer room to which intercessors can go physically day or night to pray. Most often, however, these Walls are made up of people who sign up for one or more hours per week in an organized manner until all the hours are covered in a given area or region. A successful Wall of Prayer has one or more coordinators who are responsible for signing up intercessors as well as feeding them specific prayer targets related to their community, nation, and the world.

Harmonious Prayer

One key characteristic of this movement of "Walls of Prayer" is that participants in a specific Wall function in harmonious agreement over prayer assignments provided to them by the leadership of their specific Wall. The purpose of this 31-day guide is to help strengthen this process by providing daily guidelines that are biblically based and culturally relevant. One of Christ's greatest promises regarding prayer is found in Matthew 18:19. It concerns the power of agreement in prayer: "I also tell you this: If two of you agree here on earth concerning anything you ask, my Father in heaven will do it for you" (NLT).

The Message Bible paraphrases this as follows: "When two of you get together on anything at all on earth and make a prayer of it, my Father in heaven goes into action."

An Army in Agreement!

If this promise of Christ applies to just two people praying in agreement, imagine what might happen if hundreds of people in a city or region were in daily agreement over issues close to the heart of God, like the harvest of lost souls. At present, many thousands of copies of this guide are being distributed monthly throughout the world for praying watchmen. Imagine what could happen if all those followers of Jesus were praying in daily agreement over the specific promises from God's Word on the pages that follow as they focus on critical needs of society today. This would indeed be an "army in agreement" that could change the world.

The pages of this guide include a systematic listing of such biblical focuses (promises from God) that each of those on a Wall of Prayer can agree over each time he or she prays. When you apply these promises specifically to your church, local and national governments, families, the marketplace, media, and other issues pertinent to where you live, you can imagine how tremendous the unity and harmony will be as the result of such praying. Keep in mind when you pray that thousands of other believers are praying during that very hour, in different time zones throughout the world, all agreeing over these same promises and focuses. Each daily section of this guide also provides space for you to personalize these daily focuses so they apply even more directly to your community and circumstances. Of course, we should always ask the Holy Spirit to lead us to pray even more specifically each time we keep our appointment as a watchman on our local Wall of Prayer.

A Multiplying Movement!

How fast is this movement presently multiplying? East Asia is one exciting example. At the time of this guide going to press, many new Walls of Prayer have been launched across that continent in little more than 12 months. Fifty were launched in a single 30-day period in one region. A leader of one movement in Asia reported that at the rate of Walls of Prayer rising up through their churches, their network alone would have even more complete Walls of 24/7 prayer in just 12 months. Another unrelated group has begun 24/7 prayer (with every hour filled) in 632 cities across Asia using principles shared in this guide. Similar 24/7 movements are spreading across Latin America and Africa. The 24/7 prayer movement for youth born in the United Kingdom now has spread to more than 100 nations. A movement to begin "Prayer Furnaces" (24/7 prayer) on college campuses in America has spread to many U.S. campuses.

With all this happening globally, one might ask why more prayer is needed. The best response I've heard to that question came from South African prayer leader Bennie Mostert who answered that question recently before a large congress on evangelism in Asia: "Because it's not enough!"

The Chief Thing!

I couldn't agree more. The task of gathering in and preserving the greatest harvest of souls in the history of the Church will necessitate the greatest prayer movement in the history of the Church. And that's why I welcome you as one more determined and disciplined watchman who will join the ranks of multitudes of other faithful watchmen globally. If you are both a watchman and a prayer leader, I urge you to build a Wall of Prayer even if it requires many months to establish a complete Wall. Keep in mind that a Wall of Prayer doesn't necessarily mean 24/7 "on-site" prayer, but people keeping their watch faithfully wherever they are. They do this in order that continuous prayer will rise day and night in a particular community or region. Of course, on-site prayer can be a part of this, and whenever such is possible it is highly recommended and encouraged.

As you begin your role as a watchman I challenge you with the words of two great intercessors from past generations. S. D. Gordon, a Bible teacher a century ago in Boston, declared, "The great people of the earth are the people who pray. Prayer isn't the only thing, but it is the chief thing." To this we add the provocative statement of inspired devotional writer Oswald Chambers: "Prayer isn't merely preparation for the work. Prayer is the work!"

Let's get to work!

Dick Eastman
International President
Every Home for Christ

Acknowledgements

"Withhold not good from them to whom it is due, when it is in the power of thine hand to do it" (Proverbs 3:27, KJV).

Thank you Phil Bennett for imparting the vision of Walls of Prayer into my life and ministry. The fruit of your seed is multiplying globally.

I also gratefully acknowledge Andrew Winger for his gifted design of the cover and overall layout of the chapters; and Marie Housman for her administration over the publishing of this guide. To this I add a special thank you to Jordan Middlebrook, who wrote the wonderful sample prayers to accompany the Scripture passages for each day's prayer focus.

Praying God's Promises as Watchmen on the Wall!

(To Pray God's Promises Is to Pray God's Will!)

"O Jerusalem, I have posted watchmen on your walls; they will pray to the Lord day and night for the fulfillment of his promises. Take no rest, all you who pray" (Isaiah 62:6, NLT).

"Now this is the confidence that we have in Him, that if we ask anything according to His will [as revealed in His Word], He hears us" (1 John 5:14).

Two phrases from the above verses become the basis for the use of this daily guide. Note the expression "pray...for fulfillment of his promises" (Isaiah 62:6) and "ask anything according to His will" (1 John 5:14).

Each daily focus in this guide is based upon specific promise-passages from God's Word that we can all agree upon for their fulfillment on that given day of the month over local, national, and global needs. And as we pray God's Word we are clearly praying His will. Indeed, there is no greater way to be assured of praying the will of God than to "pray His promises" back to Him. Here's a simple several-step plan to do this:

First, read the promise for a given day aloud. Read it as if God were speaking it to you personally from His throne room in heaven.

Second, turn the various phrases of that passage into prayers. Be creative as you pray that passage "back to the Lord."

Third, look for ways to apply this promise to specific situations or circumstances related to the focuses listed for that specific day. Meditate for a few moments on that passage and "watch and pray." To "watch" in prayer involves allowing the Holy Spirit to show you different ways to apply the passage to particular needs that may come to your mind.

Fourth, be careful not to let any of these promises become "stale" by thinking, "I've already prayed this passage before." Remember, God's Word is timeless and never-changing. A promise you prayed a month ago that appears in this guide is just as alive and fresh the next time you use it as if you were reading and praying it for the first time. It is also just as needed and appropriate today as it was a month ago when you last turned it into a prayer of intercession.

Finally, as you continue to use this tool from month to month think of other appropriate promises from God's Word that you can add in the extra space provided for each day so you can personalize this guide. Because God's Word is so vital to our growth in Christ, we should devote a time daily to reading the Scriptures—even apart from using this guide—for focused prayer. I recommend using a plan that takes you through the Bible in a year by reading several chapters each day. Such guides can be found on the Internet or in Christian bookstores. However, even without such a plan, by simply reading for approximately 15 minutes a day (starting in Genesis) the average reader will finish in Revelation by the end of 12 months. During your regular times of Bible reading if you find a passage that you know is applicable to a specific focus in this guide, you can add those Scriptures to the space provided for that particular day.

In using this guide you will also note that we include certain focuses daily such as prayer for the nations (with several countries listed for each day) as well as the "seven mountains" or spheres of influence that need to be penetrated with the Gospel. By listing these different nations each day for your prayers (with the four biblical "prayer claims": open doors, open minds, open hearts, and open heavens) you can pray for every nation in each month.

Though the names of the countries change from day to day, these four "prayer claims" remain the same. This is also the case regarding praying for the seven main spheres of influence (or, as some have referred to them—the "seven mountains" of influence). These specific focuses remain the same daily, but you will have a different primary promise-passage from God's Word daily to claim over these focuses. Further, you can select one or two of these focuses specifically on any given day and concentrate more on those while still touching the others in prayer. Don't become a "slave" to the system but let the system become a "servant" to your prayer watch. Always begin each hour on the Wall by asking the Holy Spirit to lead you in specific ways as you pray.

The late Armin R. Gesswein, one of the great prayer mobilizers of the 20th century, fervently challenged pastors and leaders to transform their churches and ministries into houses and ministries of prayer. Here is an edited version of a stirring article from his latter years, and very appropriate for this guide, focusing on the secret to his prayer life.

Plead the Promises of God
By Armin R. Gesswein
Founder of Revival Prayer Fellowship, Inc.

CHANGE IN THINKING!

Early in the ministry, I had an experience which *completely changed my understanding of prayer.* What a transformation! I was called to start churches and had just discovered "prayer meeting truth" in the Book of Acts. So I started a prayer meeting—the first one I ever attended let alone led.

In came an elderly Methodist believer one night. When he prayed, I detected something new. "I have never heard praying like that," I said to myself. It was not only fervency—I had plenty of that. Heaven and earth got together at once when he prayed. There was a strange immediacy about it.

The prayer and the answer were not far apart—in fact, they were moving along together. He had it "in the bag!" so it seemed to me. The Holy Spirit was right there, in action, giving him assurance of the answer even while he was praying! When I prayed, God was "way out there," somewhere in the distance, listening. The answer, too, was in the distance, in the bye and bye, as we say.

DISCOVERY!

Eager to learn his secret, I went to see him one day. His name was Ambrose Whaley, and everyone called him "Uncle Am." He was a retired blacksmith—also a Methodist lay preacher. I soon came to the point: "Uncle Am, I would love to pray with you." At once he arose, led me outside across the driveway into a red barn, up a ladder, and into a haymow!

There, in some old hay, lay two big Bibles—one open. "What is this?" I thought. I prayed first, as I recall it. I poured out my heart, needs, burdens, wishes, aspirations, and ambitions to God. Then "Uncle Am" prayed—and there was "that difference" again. There, in that hay, on our knees, at the eyeball level, I said: "Uncle Am, what is it?...You have some kind of secret in praying...Would you mind sharing it with me?"

I was 24 then, and he was 73 (he lived to be 93), and with an eagle-look in his eyes, Uncle Am said: **"Young man, learn to plead the promises of God!"**

THAT DID IT!

My praying has never been the same since. That word completely changed my understanding of prayer. It really revolutionized it! I "saw it" as soon as he said it.

Saw what? Well—when I had previously prayed there was fervency, ambition, etc. (The Lord does not put a "perfect squelch" on these either.) *But I lacked FAITH.* As the old chorus declares, prayer is the key to heaven, but faith unlocks the door. There must be faith! Where does that faith come from? It comes from hearing...the Word of God. Scripture declares: "So then faith *comes* by hearing, and hearing by the word of God" (Romans 10:17, NKJV). Uncle Am would pray Scripture after Scripture, reminding himself of promise after promise, pleading these like a lawyer does his case—the Holy Spirit pouring into Uncle Am's heart His assurance of being heard. This elderly saint knew the promises "by the bushel." He didn't seem to need those two Bibles setting in that hay!

I soon learned that Uncle Am was a mighty intercessor. He prayed "clear through." And he did it by *praying through the Bible*. He taught me the secret of effective intercessory praying. How can I ever thank God enough for leading me to such a prayer warrior in those very early years of my ministry! *What had happened to me?* With this discovery, God gave me a new Bible. I had not yet learned how to make the Bible my prayer book. It also gave me a new motivation for Bible study. I began to "dig in!" I would now search the Scriptures...meditate...mark its many promises...memorize, memorize, memorize! There are thousands of promises: a promise for every need, burden, problem, and situation.

Young man, learn to plead the promises of God! These words of Uncle Am keep ringing in my soul all these years later!

"In Him all the promises of God are yes." (2 Corinthians 1:20, Berkeley)

D. L. Moody would say: "Tarry at a promise, and God will meet you there."

PROMISES PREDICT THE ANSWERS. They are the *molds* into which we pour our prayers. They foretell what to expect. They shape our praying. They motivate, direct, and determine our supplications.

PROMISES LIKE THESE: Call unto me, and I will answer you, and show you great and mighty things, which you do not know (Jeremiah 33:3); *And whatever things you ask in prayer, believing, you will receive* (Matthew 21:22); *If you ask anything in My name, I will do it* (John 14:14).

THIS MAKES CHRISTIAN PRAYING DIFFERENT! How? In a very real sense we pray *from the answer...with the answer in mind*. Using this method we are praying *from* the answer *to* the answer. This is the way of the Lord; this is the way of *faith*. God promises—we believe. We act on His Word. In this way answered prayer not only satisfies us; it delights the heart of God by fulfilling His own Word. And this is a most important thing with God.

EXAMPLE: Remember the old arithmetic book at school? It had all the answers in the back of the book! What a book! You waited, of course; first worked out the problem and then looked up the answer! No, let's be honest! You quickly looked back for the answer; you couldn't wait! Then you worked out the problem, *with the answer in mind.* You just sought out to match it. This is how we pray. We pray from God's promise which is His answer, and expect it to be fulfilled. Also, as with the arithmetic book, there are different answers for different problems. The Bible contains thousands of promises, and these hold the answers to our thousands of needs and prayers. They are so varied—many sizes and shapes. *With them, our praying takes on another form, and moves into God's action.* How phenomenal—the Bible becomes "My Answer Book."

HOW DOES THIS WORK? Find the promise that fits your need. The Bible is just the right size. It is as big as your every need. It's as big as your life. It's *"The Book of Life."* It has answers for every situation. The promises are life-size:

- There is a promise for that *job* you need: *But seek first the kingdom of God and His righteousness, and all these things shall be added to you* (Matthew 6:33).

- There are many promises for the *guidance* you are seeking: *For as many as are led by the Spirit of God, these are sons of God.* (Romans 8:14). Another is Philippians 4:6, 7. Consult the Lord, not horoscopes! He will answer your "requests" with "peace." His word becomes your inner green light, His go-ahead.

- Do you lack *joy*? Read Philippians. For more "faith" read Hebrews! Are you *suffering*? Study 1 and 2 Peter. Are you *tempted*? Dig into Matthew 4 and Luke 4. Need *encourage-ment*? 2 Corinthians is loaded with help. Need *healing*? James 5, and many other Scriptures, like 3 John 2. Find also the many Scriptures that spur you on to pray for and help the *poor*, the *needy*, the *fatherless*, the *widows*: like James 1:27, Psalm 41:1, Matthew 25:35, etc.

- Are you praying for *revival and renewal*? Pray 2 Corinthians 7:14, Habakkuk 3:2, Acts 2:17 and Revelation 1-3. And how about *"prayer meetings?"* Are you clear on the New Testament basis for the congregational prayer meeting? The whole Book of Acts is the result of continuous prayer.

- *On and on the Scriptures will lead us*—until we learn to do "everything by prayer and supplication, with thanksgiving" and learn to *"live...by every Word of God."* (See Philippians 4:6, 7 and Luke 4:4.) Someone has wisely said that we should never pray without reading the Bible, and we should never read the Bible without praying.

It all adds up to this: We must learn to make the Bible our prayer book!

My prayer is that these words have been helpful in strengthening your own prayer life. But even after reading it you may yet find yourself wondering what promises are in the Bible for you to "plead." Listed below are a few examples of some of the Bible promises that God has made to His children. As you read these verses, think about each verse as if it were written directly to you. When you pray, acknowledge to God that His Word is true, and that this specific truth or passage is a promise that you "claim" as His child. You will be amazed at the joy and comfort you will have when you agree with God and His Word concerning *you*!

Isaiah 41:10

Fear not, for I *am* with you; Be not dismayed, for I *am* your God. I will strengthen you, Yes, I will help you, I will uphold you with My righteous right hand.

Psalm 32:8

I will instruct you and teach you in the way you should go; I will guide you with My eye.

Hebrews 13:20-21

Now may the God of peace who brought up our Lord Jesus from the dead, that great Shepherd of the sheep, through the blood of the everlasting covenant, make you complete in every good work to do His will, working in you what is well pleasing in His sight, through Jesus Christ, to whom *be* glory forever and ever. Amen.

Romans 15:13

Now may the God of hope fill you with all joy and peace in believing, that you may abound in hope by the power of the Holy Spirit.

Psalm 23

The LORD *is* my shepherd; I shall not want. He makes me to lie down in green pastures; He leads me beside the still waters. He restores my soul; He leads me in the paths of righteousness for His name's sake. Yea, though I walk through the valley of the shadow of death, I will fear no evil; for You *are* with me; Your rod and Your staff, they comfort me. You prepare a table before me in the presence of my enemies; You anoint my head with oil; my cup runs over. Surely goodness and mercy shall follow me all the days of my life; and I will dwell in the house of the LORD forever.

+

IMPORTANT NOTE: Once you have read and understand these introductory remarks concerning the use of this guide, you'll only need to use the guide itself (beginning on page 27) from day to day.

Am I Really a Watchman?

"But let no one come into the house of the LORD except the priests and those of the Levites who serve. They may go in, for they *are* holy; but all the people shall keep the watch of the LORD" (2 Chronicles 23:6).

One of the great distortions in some teaching on the subject of prayer is that only a small group of uniquely gifted people are called to be intercessors. True, some may feel they have a specific calling to give many hours daily or weekly to intercession, and some may feel it is a "full-time" calling. But all believers who take time to pray for others are intercessors. There really should be no follower of Jesus who fails to take time on a regular basis to pray for others. *Intercession is not a calling but a discipline.*

Note the above passage from 2 Chronicles. The opening part of the verse makes it clear that some leaders do have a special calling. This is true in the Church today. Some are pastors, some teachers, some worship leaders and the like. In ancient Israel there were special classes of temple leadership like the priests and the Levites. But notice how the verse ends: *"But all the people shall keep the watch of the LORD!"*

You may not be a great Bible teacher or a gifted musician or even an elder, deacon, or usher in a church. Yet, you can be a "watchman of the Lord." Indeed, as the passage concludes—"all the people shall keep the watch of the LORD!"

When the Apostle Paul was concluding his first letter to Thessalonian believers he wrote: "Therefore let us not sleep, as others *do*, but let us watch and be sober" (1 Thessalonians 5:6).

Sadly there appear to be two classes of believers in the world: sleepers and watchers. The fact that you are reading these words indicates you desire to be a watcher.

How Do I Stand Watch as a Watchman?

"I will stand my watch and set myself on the rampart, and watch to see what He will say to me..." (Habakkuk 2:1).

"Prepare the table, set a watchman in the tower...For thus has the Lord said to me: 'Go, set a watchman, let him declare what he sees'" (Isaiah 21:5a-6).

A rampart is defined as "a wall-like ridge." Habakkuk spoke of setting himself on the rampart (or wall) to watch. Notice he said, "I will stand my watch..." He considered this a personal assignment. It was his specific time to "watch," and he was determined to be faithful.

When Isaiah said of the watchman: "let him declare what he sees" (Isaiah 21:6) he was talking about what might be described as the prophetic dimension of a watchman. A watchman in ancient times was to be constantly alert to any impending attack of the enemy and to give warning to leaders of the city if he saw something of concern. In our day this suggests that watchmen stay alert to what the Holy Spirit is saying during their watch and make what they see and hear in the spiritual realm a primary focus of their intercession.

No doubt the two great keys to serving as a watchman are summed up in the words "wait" and "worship."

More than anything else a watchman must be willing to stay in his or her position until the time of their watch is complete. The Psalmist declared, "My soul *waits* for the Lord more than those who watch for the morning—*yes, more than* those who watch for the morning" (Psalm 130:6). The word "wait" means "to stay in a place in expectation of something happening." It also means "to be ready and available." Generally speaking, most of the time one spends during a typical prayer watch will lack feelings of emotion. Faithfulness, not feelings, is the key to being a good watchman. If our "watch" happens to be late in the night we might even doze from time to time.

Don't allow this to defeat you. Simply continue praying when you wake from those moments of dozing. Most important is that you do not give up. Patience is the key to waiting.

Here is where worship is so vital. Even playing a worship CD can be helpful during one's prayer watch. Singing to the Lord also can help watchmen in their prolonged times of prayer. You can sing psalms or choruses or hymns. You can even make up your own songs based on passages of Scripture. When you sing your prayers based on God's Word we refer to it as "intercessory worship." This is an excellent way to stay alert during prayer. All the passages or promises from Scripture listed in this guide can be sung as well as prayed aloud during your prayer watch. And even if you do not have a good singing voice there is no need to worry. Only God is listening. As the great worship leader A. W. Tozer declared, "You may think you have a terrible voice, but God thinks you're an opera star!"

The very purpose of this guide is to give you a plan for each day as you stand upon your watch. If you have difficulty praying an entire hour, you might find the 12-step plan from my book *The Hour That Changes the World* helpful (see page 216). It is a biblical plan that helps a person pray an entire hour by focusing on each step for approximately five minutes. Of course, by using all the specific focuses for each day as presented in this guide, you can easily fill an hour (or much more).

When Should I Schedule My Prayer Watch?

In order to fill a complete Wall of Prayer in a church or community, some intercessors will need to set aside times of prayer during the night. This, of course, is the most difficult time to pray except perhaps for those believers who are what some describe as "night owls." These are those who have no difficulty getting up at a set time of the night to pray and then have little difficulty going back to sleep. My challenge to all intercessors who would be watchmen is to give at least two hours each week specifically to help fill a Wall of Prayer.

(Some, of course, may give an hour every day.) One of those weekly hours should be during the day and the other as part of a "night watch" (usually during the hours of midnight to 6 a.m.). It is well worth the sacrifice of setting your alarm once or twice a week for a "night watch" as you realize that there are people in desperate need as you pray at that very hour.

Keep in mind as you read these words that I am assuming all believers desire to maintain a daily devotional habit. This may not always be an hour in length, but it should occur daily. During those times you may still want to use this guide to help you touch on issues for that day even if it is not your specific assigned time to have a full hour as a watchman. Obviously, any time you pray you are, in a true sense, a watchman and the focuses in this guide are always worthy of our prayers. But in order to assure that we maintain a complete Wall of Prayer in our area, with true harmony and agreement over specific needs, we need watchmen to be faithful in keeping their assigned hours. This guide can help ensure that we are all praying for the same biblical objectives, even as we allow the Holy Spirit to show us additional focuses for prayer during any given hour. Note: You are invited to join Every Home for Christ's Global Wall of Prayer at www.EHC.org/GWOP. You can register a local or area Wall of Prayer at the same website.

What Are the Four Claims for the Nations Used in This Guide?

In addition to a main passage from Scripture for each day and the primary focuses for those days, you also will discover that for each day in this guide there is a specific Bible passage related to praying for several different nations. Then, you'll see a brief list of several nations. If you use this guide faithfully, you will pray for every nation on earth once each month. You will note that we include the population of each nation to give you an idea of the number of people in these lands as well as the estimated number of evangelical (born-again) believers. To help you pray with focus and meaning for these nations, we have noted five biblical claims each day that will help you pray for vital issues related to the harvest of lost souls in those nations. This is the plan I use daily when I pray for the nations. Of course, always ask the Holy Spirit to help you pray more specifically for these claims. The prayer claims include:

1. Claim One: Open Doors!

...So the Gospel can be freely proclaimed in a region.
"Devote yourselves to prayer...that God may open a door...so that we may proclaim...Christ" (Colossians 4:2-3, NIV).

2. Claim Two: Open Minds!

...So people will hear the Gospel with an open mind.
"I am sending you to them [the lost] to open their eyes and turn them from darkness to light" (Acts 26:17b-18a, NIV).

3. Claim Three: Open Hearts!

...So unbelievers will invite Christ into their hearts.
"For God...made his light shine in our hearts to give us the light of... Christ" (2 Corinthians 4:6, NIV).

4. Claim Four: Open Heavens!

...So the transformation of a culture may begin.

"Open up, O heavens, and pour out your righteousness. Let the earth open wide so salvation and righteousness can sprout up together" (Isaiah 45:8, NLT).

The Seven Mountains of Influence
(A Sevenfold Daily Prayer Focus)

What Are the Seven Mountains of Influence
That Need Our Daily Prayers?

In the mid-1970s God drew two visionary leaders together for a luncheon meeting in Colorado. Bill Bright, founder of Campus Crusade for Christ and Loren Cunningham, founder of Youth With A Mission were those men. As they came together each felt the Lord was revealing an important strategy necessary for impacting nations and cultures in such a manner as to initiate true transformation of a society. Little did they know they both had received the same insights. Indeed, a few weeks later in Switzerland, theologian Francis Schaeffer was to receive the identical revelation. The message was simple but profound: To impact all of a culture, people, or nation with the totality of the Gospel of Jesus Christ, every major sphere of influence had to be impacted. More specifically, this involved seven clearly defined spheres, or as some have come to define them, the Seven Mountains of Influence.

You will thus notice that each daily focus in this guide includes a brief list of these seven major areas (or mountains) of influence in our global societies. In fact, the first seven days of each month's focus in this guide begin with one of these specific "mountains" as your primary prayer focus for that day, even though it is suggested you pray for all seven during each prayer watch.

We list all seven daily because each time you are "watching" on the "Wall" there are needs to be prayed for regarding all of these spheres. You may not pray in detail for all seven every day, but you can ask the Holy Spirit to help you concentrate on any specific sphere for a given day. Of course, there are numerous sub-categories that come under these spheres, and as God reveals them to you in prayer write them down in the space provided for your personal insights each day. The seven spheres include:

1. Religion *(The Church, Ministries, and Other Faiths)*

Pray for the Holy Spirit's anointing on all churches no matter their denomination. Pray for ministries involved in evangelism and discipleship including foreign missionary activity. Pray for all faiths and religions that they will see the truth of the Gospel of Jesus Christ. Pray that Christians will be bold in their witness.

2. Family and Marriages *(Youth, Children, Marriages, etc.)*

Pray for families in general, and particularly the healing of broken relationships in marriages and families, especially among believers and those in Christian ministry. Pray for the sanctity of marriage. Pray against cultural influences that diminish the value of marriage and family.

3. Education *(All Schools, Universities, Colleges, and Educators)*

This focus involves all institutions of education, whether for the very young, when children are so easily influenced, or those studying at higher levels. Pray for teachers and educators. Pray for those you know by name. Add them to your daily prayer lists for each day. Pray also for the content of textbooks so they will reflect biblical values. Ask God to send a revival to all campuses.

4. Business *(The Marketplace)*

This focus involves praying for a spiritual awakening in the marketplace. Pray especially for Christian businessmen and women that God will use them to influence others in their professions. Pray for major corporations that they will build their companies on a foundation of high moral and ethical standards.

5. Government *(Local, National, and International)*

Pray for heads of your local, state (or province), and national government. Remember especially to intercede for the judiciary (judges) of your nation and the nations of the world. Intercede for other nations listed for each day as they appear in this guide. Include the military of these nations and law enforcement as well as other service officials, such a firefighters and civil servants.

6. Media *(The Press, Television, Internet, and Social Networking)*

Ask God to cause all aspects of the media and information technology to become a tool in His hands to change the culture around us for His honor and glory. Pray that the influence of the Internet and social networking will be used by Christians to capture a new generation of young believers. Pray that Christian values and ethics will find their way into all aspects of the media.

7. Arts and Entertainment *(Including Sports)*

This focus includes all those in any field of the arts or entertainment including sports. Some have defined this sphere as the "Celebration" sphere because it takes many such aspects into consideration. Ask God to use the influence of those who know Him in these arenas so they might impact many around them. Pray for entertainers or athletes you know by name who have a strong Christian testimony. Ask God to expand their influence.

Register your personal times of prayer by joining Every Home for Christ's...

GLOBAL WALL OF PRAYER

And register existing or new Walls of Prayer at:

www.EHC.org

31-DAY WATCHMAN GUIDE

1. DAY ONE

TODAY'S WATCHMAN FOCUS:

Religion

(The Church, Revival, and Spiritual Awakening)

Pray specifically today for your church and other churches of your community or area. As you pray through today's "promise-passages" from Scripture, apply these promises to this specific focus—Religion (and more specifically, the Church). Include churches and denominations "by name," asking God to bless them with true revival. Add any to your personal list for today that you feel especially moved to pray for more regularly. Pray specifically for revival in your church and the churches of your area and for a resulting spiritual awakening in your community so that many might come to Christ as the result. Additionally, remember people of other faiths and religions that they might experience the transforming grace of Jesus Christ.

TODAY'S PROMISE-PASSAGES

Verses or phrases for the daily focuses throughout this guide are spaced appropriately in outline form to help you "pray" through each passage more easily. The ellipses (three dots) before or after a phrase do not indicate text has been removed but are used for editorial effect. Note the shaded boxes beside the various promise-passages for each day include suggested prayers as samples of how you might turn that passage into a specific prayer for that day's theme.

Ephesians 3:14-21

For this reason I bow my knees to the Father of our Lord Jesus Christ, from whom the whole family in heaven and earth is named...

Lord, I humbly bow before you as Lord of all creation to declare your Word today in prayer...

...that He would grant you, according to the riches of His glory, to be strengthened with might through His Spirit in the inner man...

I especially pray for the Church locally and globally to be strengthened by your Spirit...

...that Christ may dwell in your hearts through faith; that you, being rooted and grounded in love...

May a new maturity sweep through the Bride of Christ everywhere, rooting and grounding your children in love...

...may be able to comprehend with all the saints what *is* the width and length and depth and height..

Help us, Lord, to comprehend the scope of all that you are and all that you have for us; I praise you for your extraordinary greatness...

...to know the love of Christ which passes knowledge; that you may be filled with all the fullness of God...

Bless your people with knowledge that passes understanding, that all who name Jesus as Savior will experience the fullness of who you are...

...Now to Him who is able to do exceedingly abundantly above all that we ask or think, according to the power that works in us...

Show us miracles in our work, O Lord, that signs and wonders would follow those who carry forth your Good News to the lost whether here or abroad...

...to Him *be* glory in the church by Christ Jesus to all generations, forever and ever. Amen.

And in all of this we will be careful to give you the glory as we praise your marvelous name!

Ephesians 1:15-23

Therefore I also, after I heard of your faith in the Lord Jesus and your love for all the saints...

Father, I am grateful for all of your saints. May each unique entity of your Body be blessed today, including specific churches and denominations in my area...

...do not cease to give thanks for you, making mention of you in my prayers...

Help me, Lord, to remember as many as I can "by name" as I pray from month to month for all of your Body. I thank you for the work they do to advance your kingdom...

...that the God of our Lord Jesus Christ, the Father of glory, may give to you the spirit of wisdom and revelation in the knowledge of Him...

Especially give leaders of churches and ministries wisdom and revelation that they might be in total alignment with your perfect will in all they do...

...the eyes of your understanding being enlightened; that you may know what is the hope of His calling, what are the riches of the glory of His inheritance in the saints...

And toward this end, enlighten their eyes with supernatural sight as you draw them nearer to yourself, filling them with fresh hope for the challenges of the hour...

...and what *is* the exceeding greatness of His power toward us who believe, according to the working of His mighty power...

Reveal yourself, Lord, to those who do not know you and those of non-Christian religions. May the Good News reach many this very day...

...which He worked in Christ when He raised Him from the dead and seated *Him* at His right hand in the heavenly *places*...

Let those of other faiths see the power of the resurrection and how this reality separates all other belief systems from the uniqueness of Christ...

...far above all principality and power and might and dominion, and every name that is named, not only in this age but also in that which is to come...

Cause those of other faiths who hear or read the Gospel today to have their eyes opened supernaturally to recognize the awesome power of the living Christ...

...And He put all *things* under His feet, and gave Him *to be* head over all *things* to the church which is His body, the fullness of Him who fills all in all.

Joyfully I bring these requests before you for the Church as well as those of other faiths and religions, acknowledging that you are, indeed, the head of the Church.

PRAY GOD'S WORD OVER THE SEVEN SPHERES OF INFLUENCE:

1. Religion
   (The Church, Ministries, and Other Faiths)

2. Family and Marriages
   (Youth, Children, and the Sanctity of Marriage)

3. Education
   (All Schools, Universities, and Colleges)

4. Business
   (The Marketplace)

5. Government
   (Locally, Nationally, and Internationally)

6. Media
   (The Press, Television, Internet, and Social Networking)

7. Arts and Entertainment
   (Including Sports)

PRAY THE "FOUR CLAIMS" OVER TODAY'S NATIONS

1. Claim... **Open Doors**   (Colossians 4:2-3).
2. Claim... **Open Minds**   (Acts 26:17b-18a).
3. Claim... **Open Hearts**   (2 Corinthians 4:6).
4. Claim... **Open Heavens**   (Isaiah 45:8).

Note: Visit www.EHC.org for real-time prayer requests from the front lines of world evangelism.

TODAY'S PROMISE FOR THE NATIONS
Psalm 2:8 (NIV)

Ask me, and I will make the nations your inheritance, the ends of the earth your possession.

Father, I turn to the nations and intercede for the nations listed today. As a child of God, I, too, ask for the nations, that they will become the possession of Jesus...

Psalm 97:5-6 (NIV)

The mountains melt like wax before the LORD, before the Lord of all the earth. The heavens proclaim his righteousness, and all peoples see his glory.

Lord, I ask that strongholds that rise up against the Church will "melt like wax" before you. I pray that all the unreached peoples in these nations will soon receive the Good News.

TODAY'S NATIONS...

1.	South Africa	(Pop. 48,400,000)	% of Christians: 19.46%
2.	Lesotho	(Pop. 1,900,000)	% of Christians: 11.6%
3.	Swaziland	(Pop. 1,400,000)	% of Christians: 23.7%
4.	Madagascar	(Pop. 23,200,000)	% of Christians: 4.9%
5.	Reunion	(Pop. 800,000)	% of Christians: 5.21%
6.	Mauritius	(Pop. 1,300,000)	% of Christians: 8.15%
7.	Comoro Islands	(Pop. 800,000)	% of Christians: 0.24%
8.	Mozambique	(Pop. 24,700,000)	% of Christians: 9.1%

Pray for the peace of Jerusalem—Psalm 122:6.

MY ADDITIONAL PERSONAL FOCUSES
(Include your own prayer list.)

2. DAY TWO

FAMILY AND MARRIAGES

(Influencing Family Values and the Sanctity of Marriage through Prayer)

DAY 2

The main focus for your time on the Wall today is for families and marriages. Satan seems to have initiated all-out warfare on marriages in recent years, including Christian marriages and those of pastors and leaders. Satan knows that if he can destroy marriages, and thus the family, he can destroy the very fabric of any society. Pray today especially for families in distress that you know of as well as your own family. Pray for marriages of those close to you and for those of Christian leaders. Add any key families you know to your personal prayer list for today. As with the other focuses that begin this monthly prayer calendar, this focus is also included daily as a part of the "seven mountains" of prayer influence. We highlight it specifically here so you see how important it is to pray for this focus every day. Today you will want to concentrate extra time on this specific need. And remember, if you use this guide daily, there are many thousands of intercessors who are agreeing with you over this same focus today as you pray.

TODAY'S PROMISE-PASSAGES

Ephesians 5:25-33

Husbands, love your wives, just as Christ also loved the church and gave Himself for her, that He might sanctify and cleanse her with the washing of water by the word...

Father, I come to you on behalf of families everywhere and ask you to bless fathers and husbands, particularly in Christian homes, that they might honor their wives and live a life of true godliness in Christ...

...that He might present her to Himself a glorious church, not having spot or wrinkle or any such thing, but that she should be holy and without blemish...

Lord, just as you long for a glorious Church without "spot or wrinkle" we desire this same picture for families: pure and living in harmony with your Word...

...so husbands ought to love their own wives as their own bodies; he who loves his wife loves himself...

Give husbands a deep love for their wives that brings you honor in the Church and the community at large...

...For no one ever hated his own flesh, but nourishes and cherishes it, just as the Lord *does* the church...

Teach husbands and wives what it means to nourish and cherish each other in a way that mirrors the unity in the Trinity...

...For we are members of His body, of His flesh and of His bones...

Remind us, O Lord, that we are a part of your glorious Body and in honoring each other we are honoring you...

..."*For this reason a man shall leave his father and mother and be joined to his wife, and the two shall become one flesh*"...

Remind us that in a marriage in Christ a supernatural work has occurred, causing us to become "one flesh." May we care for each other as we would want to care for ourselves...

...This is a great mystery, but I speak concerning Christ and the church...

Lord, reveal yourself in marriages and families, that we might manifest the harmony you long for in the Church...

...Nevertheless let each one of you in particular so love his own wife as himself, and let the wife *see* that she respects *her* husband.

Lord, fill our homes and families with love and respect for each other so that we might give you joy and bring you glory.

Mark 10:1-9

Then He arose from there and came to the region of Judea by the other side of the Jordan. And multitudes gathered to Him again, and as He was accustomed, He taught them again. The Pharisees came and asked Him, "Is it lawful for a man to divorce *his* wife?" testing Him...

Father, we know that you are deeply concerned about the health of families and that throughout history the issue of divorce has troubled you...

...And He answered and said to them, "What did Moses command you?" They said, "Moses permitted *a man* to write a certificate of divorce, and to dismiss *her.*" And Jesus answered and said to them, "Because of the hardness of your heart he wrote you this precept...

We know, O Lord, the break-up of families always begins with the hardness of hearts toward your will and your ways...

...But from the beginning of the creation, God *'made them male and female.' 'For this reason a man shall leave his father and mother and be joined to his wife, and the two shall become one flesh';* so then they are no longer two, but one flesh. Therefore what God has joined together, let not man separate."

Restore families, I pray, by drawing them closer to you "as one in you" and into your Word so they might know your plans and purposes for a healthy home. I pray that attacks on marriage and the family in the culture of today will be reversed through a revival of purity, holiness, and a return to biblical family values.

Genesis 18:17-19

And the LORD said, "Shall I hide from Abraham what I am doing, since Abraham shall surely become a great and mighty nation, and all the nations of the earth shall be blessed in him?...

Father, we know that it is your desire to bless families just as you promised Abraham in ancient times...

...For I have known him, in order that he may command his children and his household after him, that they keep the way of the LORD, to do righteousness and justice, that the LORD may bring to Abraham what He has spoken to him."

Finally, I pray that more Christian parents will teach their children godly principles, firmly based in your Word, so that they may grow up keeping all your ways in righteousness and justice.

PRAY GOD'S WORD OVER
THE SEVEN SPHERES OF INFLUENCE:

1. **Religion**
   (The Church, Ministries, and Other Faiths)

2. **Family and Marriages**
   (Youth, Children, and the Sanctity of Marriage)

3. **Education**
   (All Schools, Universities, and Colleges)

4. **Business**
   (The Marketplace)

5. **Government**
   (Locally, Nationally, and Internationally)

6. **Media**
   (The Press, Television, Internet, and Social Networking)

7. **Arts and Entertainment**
   (Including Sports)

PRAY THE "FOUR CLAIMS" OVER
TODAY'S NATIONS

1. Claim... **Open Doors** (Colossians 4:2-3).
2. Claim... **Open Minds** (Acts 26:17b-18a).
3. Claim... **Open Hearts** (2 Corinthians 4:6).
4. Claim... **Open Heavens** (Isaiah 45:8).

**Note: Visit www.EHC.org for real-time prayer requests
from the front lines of world evangelism.**

TODAY'S PROMISE FOR THE NATIONS

Psalm 47:1-3 (NIV)

Clap your hands, all you nations; shout to God with cries of joy. For the LORD Most High is awesome, the great King over all the earth...

Father, I rejoice in you today for all that you are doing in the nations. You are, indeed, truly awesome and great in every way, and I declare your greatness over the nations on my watchman list today...

...He subdued nations under us, peoples under our feet.

May all the dark powers of evil be subdued in these nations in order that many might come to know Christ as Savior in these very lands this day!

TODAY'S NATIONS...

1.	Zimbabwe	(Pop. 13,800,000)	% of Christians: 26.22%
2.	Botswana	(Pop. 2,200,000)	% of Christians: 7.98%
3.	Namibia	(Pop. 2,200,000)	% of Christians: 12.49%
4.	St. Helena	(Pop. 7,776)	% of Christians: 8.80%
5.	Angola	(Pop. 19,100,000)	% of Christians: 22.72%
6.	Zambia	(Pop. 14,600,000)	% of Christians: 21.04%
7.	Malawi	(Pop. 17,400,000)	% of Christians: 16.2%

Pray for the peace of Jerusalem—Psalm 122:6.

MY ADDITIONAL PERSONAL FOCUSES
(Include your own prayer list.)

_____

_____

_____

_____

_____

_____

_____

_____

_____

_____

_____

_____

_____

_____

_____

_____

_____

_____

_____

3. DAY THREE

EDUCATION

(All Institutions of Learning, Teachers, and Administrators)

This is another of the seven main focuses that we encourage you to pray for daily. Again, as with the other six focuses that begin this monthly guide, today you will take extra time to pray more in-depth for the education focus. This involves all levels of education from younger children in elementary school, through more advanced education, including college and university students. Pray for an awakening among students of all ages as well as for their teachers. When possible pray "by name" for those students and teachers you know. Pray also that godly principles will come into the curriculum being taught at all levels of education.

DAY 3

TODAY'S PROMISE-PASSAGES

Ecclesiastes 12:9-14

And moreover, because the Preacher was wise, he still taught the people knowledge; yes, he pondered and sought out *and* set in order many proverbs...

Father, we know that you are the author of all true knowledge and that it is you who gave humankind the ability to acquire that knowledge...

...The Preacher sought to find acceptable words; and *what was* written *was* upright—words of truth...

We also know, O Lord, that some knowledge can bring great good, and some can be used to cause much evil...

...The words of the wise are like goads, and the words of scholars are like well-driven nails, given by one Shepherd...

Thank you, Lord, for those who are involved in the process of education committed to teaching your righteous ways...

...And further, my son, be admonished by these. Of making many books *there is* no end, and much study *is* wearisome to the flesh...

I pray today especially for the content of textbooks that school systems use to educate our youth. May those who author and compile these texts overcome any bias that may distort the truth...

...Let us hear the conclusion of the whole matter: Fear God and keep His commandments, for this is man's all...

And may students everywhere, even in ungodly settings, come to realize ultimately that all true knowledge finds its fulfillment and purpose only in the reverence of you, our creator...

...For God will bring every work into judgment, including every secret thing, whether good or evil.

I also ask, O Lord, that you would judge institutions of education and those who lead them, that they would see the worth and necessity of creating a climate of righteousness and justice as foundational to all they impart to their students.

Proverbs 1:5-9

A wise *man* will hear and increase learning, and a man of understanding will attain wise counsel, to understand a proverb and an enigma, the words of the wise and their riddles...

...The fear of the LORD *is* the beginning of knowledge, *but* fools despise wisdom and instruction...

...My son, hear the instruction of your father, and do not forsake the law of your mother...

...For they *will be* a graceful ornament on your head, and chains about your neck.

Lord, I further ask that you will give us wise and righteous teachers and professors at all levels of learning, opening doors especially for Christian educators to expand their influences...

Reveal to these educators that the true source of knowledge can only be found in understanding your ways and purposes through the fear and reverence for who you are...

I pray further for students of all ages to discover these realities and that a revival among the youth of our land will sweep through our many institutions of learning...

Finally, O Lord, raise up bands of praying students on campuses everywhere, both here and in other lands, who will seek you, even day and night, for an awakening on campuses everywhere.

PRAY GOD'S WORD OVER
THE SEVEN SPHERES OF INFLUENCE:

1. Religion
   (The Church, Ministries, and Other Faiths)

2. Family and Marriages
   (Youth, Children, and the Sanctity of Marriage)

3. Education
   (All Schools, Universities, and Colleges)

4. Business
   (The Marketplace)

5. Government
   (Locally, Nationally, and Internationally)

6. Media
   (The Press, Television, Internet, and Social Networking)

7. Arts and Entertainment
   (Including Sports)

PRAY THE "FOUR CLAIMS" OVER
TODAY'S NATIONS

1. Claim... **Open Doors** (Colossians 4:2-3).

2. Claim... **Open Minds** (Acts 26:17b-18a).

3. Claim... **Open Hearts** (2 Corinthians 4:6).

4. Claim... **Open Heavens** (Isaiah 45:8).

Note: Visit www.EHC.org for real-time prayer requests from the front lines of world evangelism.

TODAY'S PROMISE FOR THE NATIONS

Psalm 33:10-11 (NIV)

The LORD foils the plans of the nations; he thwarts the purposes of the peoples...

Lord, as I prepare to pray for the nations on today's list I first of all praise you for the way you are already working in these nations to foil the plans of all satanic forces...

...But the plans of the LORD stand firm forever, the purposes of his heart through all generations.

I declare over these nations that your plans and purposes to redeem multitudes from each of them will be fulfilled and that you will anoint your remnant in these nations as they proclaim the truth of the Gospel everywhere.

TODAY'S NATIONS...

1.	Tanzania	(Pop. 49,600,000)	% of Christians: 10.04%
2.	Rwanda	(Pop. 12,300,000)	% of Christians: 22.11%
3.	Burundi	(Pop. 10,400,000)	% of Christians: 27.34%
4.	Dem. Rep. of Congo	(Pop. 77,400,000)	% of Christians: 19.44%
5.	Republic of Congo	(Pop. 4,700,000)	% of Christians: 15.26%
6.	Gabon	(Pop. 1,700,000)	% of Christians: 12.29%
7.	São Tome & Principe	(Pop. 200,000)	% of Christians: 4.8%

Pray for the peace of Jerusalem—Psalm 122:6.

MY ADDITIONAL PERSONAL FOCUSES
(Include your own prayer list.)

_____

_____

_____

_____

_____

_____

_____

_____

_____

_____

_____

_____

_____

_____

_____

_____

_____

4. DAY FOUR

TODAY'S WATCHMAN FOCUS:

BUSINESS

(The Influence of the Marketplace)

Today's primary focus is also something that should be a part of our prayers daily. However, today we will focus even more time on the area of business and the marketplace. Pray for businesses in your community or nation that God will use them to accomplish His purposes. Ask God to raise up godly businessmen and women to be witnesses for Him wherever they serve. Apply today's "promise-passage" of Scripture specifically to the marketplace. Pray that God will release funds from businesses in your area and throughout the world to make possible the advancement of Christ's kingdom and the completion of the Great Commission.

DAY 4

TODAY'S PROMISE-PASSAGES

Isaiah 60:1-6

Arise, shine; for your light has come! And the glory of the LORD is risen upon you. For behold, the darkness shall cover the earth, and deep darkness the people; But the LORD will arise over you, and His glory will be seen upon you...

Father, today I bring before you the businesses and marketplace of my nation and around the world. Business is an influential sector in our world, and I pray that you would use it for your purposes. Make businesses in my community vessels for your will and work...

...The Gentiles shall come to your light, and kings to the brightness of your rising. "Lift up your eyes all around, and see: They all gather together, they come to you; Your sons shall come from afar, and your daughters shall be nursed at *your* side...

...I pray, Lord, that you would appoint and raise up godly businessmen and women who would follow you in all of their activities. Let Christian leadership, management, and employees be strong witnesses of you in the marketplace, drawing the world's powerful and influential people to you...

...Then you shall see and become radiant, and your heart shall swell with joy; because the abundance of the sea shall be turned to you, the wealth of the Gentiles shall come to you...

...I ask that you would bless godly businesses so that others in the marketplace would be attracted to your ways. Father, pour out your blessings on those who truly follow you. Make the wonders of your name known through them...

...The multitude of camels shall cover your *land*, the dromedaries of Midian and Ephah; all those from Sheba shall come; they shall bring gold and incense, and they shall proclaim the praises of the LORD.

...And teach godly businessmen and women to give you glory in all their endeavors. Make godly businesses an example to the marketplace and to the world of your love and holiness.

Deuteronomy 8:18-20

"And you shall remember the LORD your God, for *it is* He who gives you power to get wealth, that He may establish His covenant which He swore to your fathers, as *it is* this day...

I pray, Lord, that your hand would be involved in the marketplace of my nation. Reveal yourself as the source of all wealth so that businessmen and women would recognize you as the one true God.

...Then it shall be, if you by any means forget the LORD your God, and follow other gods, and serve them and worship them, I testify against you this day that you shall surely perish...

I pray against all corruption and greed in the marketplace, Lord. Let business practices be fair and honest. Teach business leaders your ways and convict their hearts with your truth...

...As the nations which the LORD destroys before you, so you shall perish, because you would not be obedient to the voice of the LORD your God."

...And use businesses to fund the work of ministry, Father. Give businessmen and women generous hearts, and prosper businesses that use their resources to sow into your kingdom.

PRAY GOD'S WORD OVER THE SEVEN SPHERES OF INFLUENCE:

1. **Religion**
   (The Church, Ministries, and Other Faiths)

2. **Family and Marriages**
   (Youth, Children, and the Sanctity of Marriage)

3. **Education**
   (All Schools, Universities, and Colleges)

4. **Business**
   (The Marketplace)

5. **Government**
   (Locally, Nationally, and Internationally)

6. **Media**
   (The Press, Television, Internet, and Social Networking)

7. **Arts and Entertainment**
   (Including Sports)

PRAY THE "FOUR CLAIMS" OVER TODAY'S NATIONS

1. Claim... **Open Doors**   (Colossians 4:2-3).
2. Claim... **Open Minds**   (Acts 26:17b-18a).
3. Claim... **Open Hearts**   (2 Corinthians 4:6).
4. Claim... **Open Heavens**   (Isaiah 45:8).

Note: Visit www.EHC.org for real-time prayer requests from the front lines of world evangelism.

TODAY'S PROMISE FOR THE NATIONS

Psalm 45:5-6 (NIV)

Let your sharp arrows pierce the hearts of the king's enemies; let the nations fall beneath your feet. Your throne, O God, will last for ever and ever; a scepter of justice will be the scepter of your kingdom.

And now, O Lord, I pray for the nations. I declare your glory over these seven nations on my list and pray that the peoples of each country would fall before you in worship. Let their hearts be turned to you for eternity, Father.

TODAY'S NATIONS...

1.	Equatorial Guinea	(Pop. 700,000)	% of Christians: 4.55%
2.	Cameroon	(Pop. 23,100,000)	% of Christians: 8.46%
3.	Central African Rep.	(Pop. 5,300,000)	% of Christians: 33.71%
4.	Uganda	(Pop. 36,00,000)	% of Christians: 31.34%
5.	Kenya	(Pop. 45,000,000)	% of Christians: 41.5%
6.	Somalia	(Pop. 10,400,000)	% of Christians: 0.01%
7.	Ethiopia	(Pop. 96,600,000)	% of Christians: 17.26%

Pray for the peace of Jerusalem—Psalm 122:6.

MY ADDITIONAL PERSONAL FOCUSES
(Include your own prayer list.)

5. DAY FIVE

TODAY'S WATCHMAN FOCUS:

GOVERNMENT

(Local, National, and International Governments)

The Apostle Paul instructed Timothy in his first letter to this young leader to "pray for all that are in authority" (1 Timothy 2:1-2). There is little doubt that Paul's first concern in this regard was for prayer that impacted those in government positions. Pray for your local government leaders as well as for those of your nation, whether it be a president, prime minister, or other ruling authority. As God leads you, include leaders of other nations as well. You will notice that this focus is a part of each day's "Watchman Prayer Strategy" as it is one of the primary "seven mountains" of authority. Even though you will pray for all seven of these mountains daily, today we want to focus extra time in prayer on those involved in government.

DAY 5

TODAY'S PROMISE-PASSAGES

Romans 13:1-7

Let every soul be subject to the governing authorities. For there is no authority except from God, and the authorities that exist are appointed by God. Therefore whoever resists the authority resists the ordinance of God, and those who resist will bring judgment on themselves...

Father, today I intercede on behalf of the government. I lift up the government in my local community, in my nation, and in nations around the world. I pray that every government position would be held by a leader chosen and appointed by you...

...For rulers are not a terror to good works, but to evil. Do you want to be unafraid of the authority? Do what is good, and you will have praise from the same...

...I pray, Lord, for moral proceedings in all levels of government. Direct government leaders to protect what is good and to fight against what is evil...

...For he is God's minister to you for good. But if you do evil, be afraid; for he does not bear the sword in vain; for he is God's minister, an avenger to execute wrath on him who practices evil...

...Guard the hearts and minds of government leaders, Father. Keep their hands from corruption and bribery. Let them stand for truth and pursue the good of the people they represent. Have your hand in the process of elections and appointments.

...Therefore *you* must be subject, not only because of wrath but also for conscience' sake. For because of this you also pay taxes, for they are God's ministers attending continually to this very thing...

I pray that you would establish order in nations where there is political unrest. Raise up godly leaders and replace government officials who inflict oppression. Use all levels of government to accomplish the things of your will...

...Render therefore to all their due: taxes to whom taxes *are due,* customs to whom customs, fear to whom fear, honor to whom honor.

...Teach me to respect and honor those in government authority over me, Father. Show me how to glorify you in my interaction with my local and national government.

1 Timothy 2:1-4

Therefore I exhort first of all that supplications, prayers, intercessions, *and* giving of thanks be made for all men, for kings and all who are in authority, that we may lead a quiet and peaceable life in all godliness and reverence...

...For this *is* good and acceptable in the sight of God our Savior, who desires all men to be saved and to come to the knowledge of the truth.

Lord, I pray that the local and national governments of my nation would promote peace in my community. I pray by name for government officials I know and ask that you would fill them with the knowledge of your will...

...I pray especially for the salvation of my government leaders. Let your Gospel go forth in local, national, and international governments so that the world might be transformed.

PRAY GOD'S WORD OVER
THE SEVEN SPHERES OF INFLUENCE:

1. Religion
   (The Church, Ministries, and Other Faiths)

2. Family and Marriages
   (Youth, Children, and the Sanctity of Marriage)

3. Education
   (All Schools, Universities, and Colleges)

4. Business
   (The Marketplace)

5. Government
   (Locally, Nationally, and Internationally)

6. Media
   (The Press, Television, Internet, and Social Networking)

7. Arts and Entertainment
   (Including Sports)

PRAY THE "FOUR CLAIMS" OVER
TODAY'S NATIONS

1. Claim... **Open Doors** (Colossians 4:2-3).
2. Claim... **Open Minds** (Acts 26:17b-18a).
3. Claim... **Open Hearts** (2 Corinthians 4:6).
4. Claim... **Open Heavens** (Isaiah 45:8).

Note: Visit www.EHC.org for a more specific daily prayer focus for world evangelism.

TODAY'S PROMISE FOR THE NATIONS

Psalm 22:27-28 (NIV)

All the ends of the earth will remember and turn to the LORD, and all the families of the nations will bow down before him, for dominion belongs to the LORD and he rules over the nations.

Lord, I pray that the knowledge of who you are and what you have done would spread across these nations on my list today. I lift them up and ask that you would draw all families to you. I declare your sovereignty over each of these nations!

TODAY'S NATIONS...

1.	Eritrea	(Pop. 6,400,000)	% of Christians: 2.14%
2.	Djibouti	(Pop. 800,000)	% of Christians: 0.06%
3.	South Sudan	(Pop. 11,600,000)	% of Christians: 11.51%
4.	Sudan	(Pop. 35,500,000)	% of Christians: .39%
5.	Chad	(Pop. 11,400,000)	% of Christians: 11.01%
6.	Nigeria	(Pop. 177,200,000)	% of Christians: 19.69%
7.	Niger	(Pop. 17,500,000)	% of Christians: 0.14%

Pray for the peace of Jerusalem—Psalm 122:6.

MY ADDITIONAL PERSONAL FOCUSES
(Include your own prayer list.)

_____

_____

_____

_____

_____

_____

_____

_____

_____

_____

_____

_____

_____

_____

_____

_____

_____

_____

6. DAY SIX

TODAY'S WATCHMAN FOCUS:

MEDIA

(Radio, Television, Print, Internet, and Social Networking)

The impact of all forms of media in our various cultures cannot be overemphasized. Whether it is the print media (newspapers or magazines), television, radio, or the rapidly spreading influence of the Internet and all forms of social networking, media should be an object of our daily prayers. This is why you will see this on our daily list for focused prayer as one of the "seven mountains" of influence. Today we will take added time to concentrate our prayers specifically on this vital focus. Pray that God will use publishers of newspapers and magazines as well as Internet websites to report in such a manner that is ethically and morally sound. Ask that God will redeem the media to advance His kingdom. Claim the same for the television industry. Ask that God will continue to use radio in a significant way to spread the Gospel globally. Especially pray for the growing influence of the Internet and social networking. Pray against the spread of pornography on the Internet and that God will cause those who "surf" the Internet to come upon godly websites that draw them to salvation in Jesus Christ.

TODAY'S PROMISE-PASSAGES

Ephesians 2:1-7

And you *He made alive*, who were dead in trespasses and sins in which you once walked according to the course of this world, according to the prince of the power of the air, the spirit who now works in the sons of disobedience...

Father, we know that the enemy uses the media to deceive the world and to draw your children into sinfulness. Television, newspapers, and the Internet seem to be infiltrated with impurity, darkness, and death...

...among whom also we all once conducted ourselves in the lusts of our flesh, fulfilling the desires of the flesh and of the mind, and were by nature children of wrath, just as the others...

I know that before you saved me, I was entrapped in those same transgressions and caught in that darkness. I was a slave to the desires of my flesh, and I deserved your wrath...

...But God, who is rich in mercy, because of His great love with which He loved us, even when we were dead in trespasses, made us alive together with Christ (by grace you have been saved)...

...But you redeemed me even when I was dead in my sins. You made me alive in Christ through your saving power. Thank you! Father, I ask that you would bring that redemptive power to the media.

...and raised *us* up together, and made *us* sit together in the heavenly *places* in Christ Jesus, that in the ages to come He might show the exceeding riches of His grace in *His* kindness toward us in Christ Jesus.

O Lord, would you, in your sovereignty, purify all forms of media so that the things the world sees, hears, reads, and watches would be glorifying to you. I ask that you would use the media as your tool to show the world the riches of your grace and kindness.

Mark 7:17-23

When He had entered a house away from the crowd, His disciples asked Him concerning the parable. So He said to them, "Are you thus without understanding also? Do you not perceive that whatever enters a man from outside cannot defile him, because it does not enter his heart but his stomach, and is eliminated, *thus* purifying all foods?"...

...And He said, "What comes out of a man, that defiles a man. For from within, out of the heart of men, proceed evil thoughts, adulteries, fornications, murders, thefts, covetousness, wickedness, deceit, lewdness, an evil eye, blasphemy, pride, foolishness. All these evil things come from within and defile a man."

Father, I understand that the things I watch, see, and hear are not the same as the things I take into my body when I eat. The things I eat are temporary, but the things of the media that I allow to enter my life become seeds in my heart and mind that grow and produce fruit—either good or evil— that will be evident in my life...

...O Lord, help me guard my heart and mind against all evil and impurity in the media. I do not want my life to bear the fruit of such wickedness and deceit. And Father, I ask that you would take hold of all forms of media and cause them to be vessels of your light and life.

PRAY GOD'S WORD OVER THE SEVEN SPHERES OF INFLUENCE:

1. Religion
   (The Church, Ministries, and Other Faiths)

2. Family and Marriages
   (Youth, Children, and the Sanctity of Marriage)

3. Education
   (All Schools, Universities, and Colleges)

4. Business
   (The Marketplace)

5. Government
   (Locally, Nationally, and Internationally)

6. Media
   (The Press, Television, Internet, and Social Networking)

7. Arts and Entertainment
   (Including Sports)

PRAY THE "FOUR CLAIMS" OVER TODAY'S NATIONS

1. Claim... **Open Doors** (Colossians 4:2-3).
2. Claim... **Open Minds** (Acts 26:17b-18a).
3. Claim... **Open Hearts** (2 Corinthians 4:6).
4. Claim... **Open Heavens** (Isaiah 45:8).

Note: Visit www.EHC.org for real-time prayer requests from the front lines of world evangelism.

TODAY'S PROMISE FOR THE NATIONS

Psalm 45:17 (NIV)

I will perpetuate your memory through all generations; therefore the nations will praise you for ever and ever.

O Lord, use your people to make your name and your great deeds known in all the nations on my list today. Let young and old in these nations worship you because of the testimony of who you are!

TODAY'S NATIONS...

1.	Benin	(Pop. 10,200,000)	% of Christians: 7.21%
2.	Togo	(Pop. 7,400,000)	% of Christians: 8.89%
3.	Ghana	(Pop. 25,800,000)	% of Christians: 19.22%
4.	Burkina Faso	(Pop. 18,400,000)	% of Christians: 9.15%
5.	Côte d'Ivoire	(Pop. 22,800,000)	% of Christians: 7.63%
6.	Liberia	(Pop. 4,100,000)	% of Christians: 9.66%
7.	Cape Verde Islands	(Pop. 500,000)	% of Christians: 6.56%

Pray for the peace of Jerusalem—Psalm 122:6.

MY ADDITIONAL PERSONAL FOCUSES
(Include your own prayer list.)

7. DAY SEVEN

TODAY'S WATCHMAN FOCUS:
ARTS AND ENTERTAINMENT (SPORTS)
(Influencing the Influencers of All Forms of Entertainment)

Related to yesterday's primary focus (the media) are the areas of the arts, entertainment, and sports. Praise God for the growing number of famous entertainers and sports personalities who have professed Christ as Savior. Pray that God will greatly expand their influence. As is the case with the other primary "spheres of influence" that begin this 31-day guide, arts, entertainment, and sports are focuses that are worthy of your daily prayers. These areas clearly represent a "mountain of influence" in most cultures. Use today's "promise-passage" to claim God's presence in the entertainment industry and sports in our nations and throughout the world. Ask God to raise up more anointed Christian spokespersons (men and women) in all areas of sports and entertainment. Pray also that God will open the eyes of those who are impacted by the entertainment industry (or sports) to recognize when they are being led astray by ungodly influences.

TODAY'S PROMISE-PASSAGES

Ephesians 4:17-24

This I say, therefore, and testify in the Lord, that you should no longer walk as the rest of the Gentiles walk, in the futility of their mind, having their understanding darkened, being alienated from the life of God, because of the ignorance that is in them, because of the blindness of their heart...

Father, I grieve with your heart over those who are separated from you because they live in darkness, the eyes of their hearts blind to you. So often, figures in the arts and entertainment industries seem lost from you, walking instead in the ways of the world...

...who, being past feeling, have given themselves over to lewdness, to work all uncleanness with greediness...

...Sometimes stubbornness against you and your ways is glorified, and the industry is often marked by an immoral quest for wealth and fame...

...But you have not so learned Christ, if indeed you have heard Him and have been taught by Him, as the truth is in Jesus: that you put off, concerning your former conduct, the old man which grows corrupt according to the deceitful lusts...

...But you, O Lord, have called us to live Christ-like lives that draw others to you, rejecting our old ways and living in holiness that marks us as yours. Father, I ask that you would help your people stand firm in holiness—especially those in the arts and entertainment industries...

...and be renewed in the spirit of your mind, and that you put on the new man which was created according to God, in true righteousness and holiness.

...Make them shining examples of your righteousness and holiness so that the world might be drawn to you through their work and performance as they reflect you.

Philippians 4:8-9

Finally, brethren, whatever things *are* true, whatever things *are* noble, whatever things *are* just, whatever things *are* pure, whatever things *are* lovely, whatever things *are* of good report, if *there is* any virtue and if *there is* anything praiseworthy—meditate on these things...

Lord, you are the creator of all things, and you have made us in your image so that we are creative like you. Today I pray that your Spirit would fill and inspire the arts and entertainment industries so that the things we create and celebrate would reflect your beauty and purity. Let creativity lead the world back to you, the creator...

...The things which you learned and received and heard and saw in me, these do, and the God of peace will be with you.

...As we create, teach us to emulate your love always, O Lord, and fill us with your peace so that we can share it with others.

PRAY GOD'S WORD OVER
THE SEVEN SPHERES OF INFLUENCE:

1. **Religion**
   (The Church, Ministries, and Other Faiths)

2. **Family and Marriages**
   (Youth, Children, and the Sanctity of Marriage)

3. **Education**
   (All Schools, Universities, and Colleges)

4. **Business**
   (The Marketplace)

5. **Government**
   (Locally, Nationally, and Internationally)

6. **Media**
   (The Press, Television, Internet, and Social Networking)

7. **Arts and Entertainment**
   (Including Sports)

PRAY THE "FOUR CLAIMS" OVER
TODAY'S NATIONS

1.	Claim... **Open Doors**	(Colossians 4:2-3).
2.	Claim... **Open Minds**	(Acts 26:17b-18a).
3.	Claim... **Open Hearts**	(2 Corinthians 4:6).
4.	Claim... **Open Heavens**	(Isaiah 45:8).

**Note: Visit www.EHC.org for real-time prayer requests
from the front lines of world evangelism.**

TODAY'S PROMISE FOR THE NATIONS

Psalm 46:10-11 (NIV)

"Be still, and know that I am God; I will be exalted among the nations, I will be exalted in the earth."...

Father, I declare that because you are the one true God, all the nations I am lifting up to you today will see and worship you...

...The LORD Almighty is with us; the God of Jacob is our fortress.

...I ask you to be with your people who love you in these nations, O Lord; protect them with your mighty arm.

TODAY'S NATIONS...

1.	Sierra Leone	(Pop. 5,700,000)	% of Christians: 3.49%
2.	Guinea	(Pop. 11,500,000)	% of Christians: 0.72%
3.	Guinea-Bissau	(Pop. 1,700,000)	% of Christians: 1.82%
4.	Senegal	(Pop. 13,600,000)	% of Christians: 0.17%
5.	Gambia	(Pop. 1,900,000)	% of Christians: 0.63%
6.	Mali	(Pop. 16,500,000)	% of Christians: 0.58%
7.	Mauritania	(Pop. 3,500,000)	% of Christians: 0.10%

Pray for the peace of Jerusalem—Psalm 122:6.

MY ADDITIONAL PERSONAL FOCUSES
(Include your own prayer list.)

_____

_____

_____

_____

_____

_____

_____

_____

_____

_____

_____

_____

_____

_____

_____

_____

_____

_____

_____

_____

8. DAY EIGHT

TODAY'S WATCHMAN FOCUS:

ISRAEL

(The Well-Being of God's Chosen People)

The nation of Israel clearly plays a pivotal role in the history and destiny of nations. The Bible includes important promises that link our blessing and prosperity as believers to how we treat Israel. We are admonished to "pray for the peace of Jerusalem" and to speak blessing on the Jewish people (Psalm 122:6-9). God said through the Prophet Zechariah, "He who touches you touches the apple of His eye" (Zechariah 2:8). In the many prophecies of Scripture that point toward end times, it is clear that Israel is a central focus in much that transpires. The apostle Paul set an example of praying for the Jewish people when he declared, "Brethren, my heart's desire and prayer to God for Israel is that they may be saved" (Romans 10:1). Today, in addition to all that we pray for during our time as watchmen, we pray for the peace of Jerusalem and seek a blessing on Jewish people everywhere. We especially pray for the eyes of God's chosen people to see the reality of their true Messiah, Jesus Christ. Pray particularly that God will strengthen Messianic Jews who are willing to endure suffering, as Paul did, for the privilege of proclaiming Jesus Christ to their fellow Jews.

TODAY'S PROMISE-PASSAGES

Psalm 122:1-9

I was glad when they said to me, "Let us go into the house of the LORD." Our feet have been standing within your gates, O Jerusalem! Jerusalem is built as a city that is compact together...

...Where the tribes go up, the tribes of the LORD, to the Testimony of Israel, to give thanks to the name of the LORD. For thrones are set there for judgment, the thrones of the house of David...

...Pray for the peace of Jerusalem: "May they prosper who love you. Peace be within your walls, Prosperity within your palaces."...

...For the sake of my brethren and companions, I will now say, "Peace *be* within you." Because of the house of the LORD our God I will seek your good.

O Lord, from the days of Abraham, you chose for yourself a people through whom you would reveal yourself to the world and draw all nations into the blessing of your family...

...But now your people, the Jewish people, are scattered across the face of the earth, and so many of them are separated from you. Father, I pray for your people today...

...I ask for the redemption and restoration of your people. Reveal yourself and your Son to the Israelites, Father, and bring them back to you...

...Because we love your family, O Lord, we ask for peace for the Jewish people. I pray that you would graft them back into your people.

Zechariah 2:10-13 (NIV)

"Shout and be glad, O daughter of Zion. For I am coming, and I will live among you," declares the Lord...

Father, I pray that your Spirit would descend on the Jewish people once again, as you have declared—that your presence would dwell among them...

..."Many nations will be joined with the Lord in that day and will become my people. I will live among you and you will know that the Lord Almighty has sent me to you...

I praise you, O Lord, that your chosen people were not chosen for exclusivity, but for the purpose of bringing all nations on earth into your family. Thank you that Jews and Gentiles alike are your people in Christ...

...The Lord will inherit Judah as his portion in the holy land and will again choose Jerusalem. Be still before the Lord, all mankind, because he has roused himself from his holy dwelling."

...Today I ask that you would open the hearts of the Israelite people to the Gospel of your Son. Call their hearts to obedience to you, and use them to reach the nations.

PRAY GOD'S WORD OVER THE SEVEN SPHERES OF INFLUENCE:

1. Religion
   (The Church, Ministries, and Other Faiths)

2. Family and Marriages
   (Youth, Children, and the Sanctity of Marriage)

3. Education
   (All Schools, Universities, and Colleges)

4. Business
   (The Marketplace)

5. Government
   (Locally, Nationally, and Internationally)

6. Media
   (The Press, Television, Internet, and Social Networking)

7. Arts and Entertainment
   (Including Sports)

PRAY THE "FOUR CLAIMS" OVER TODAY'S NATIONS

1. Claim... **Open Doors** (Colossians 4:2-3).
2. Claim... **Open Minds** (Acts 26:17b-18a).
3. Claim... **Open Hearts** (2 Corinthians 4:6).
4. Claim... **Open Heavens** (Isaiah 45:8).

Note: Visit www.EHC.org for real-time prayer requests from the front lines of world evangelism.

TODAY'S PROMISE FOR THE NATIONS

Psalm 47:7-8 (NIV)

For God is the King of all the earth; sing to him a psalm of praise. God reigns over the nations; God is seated on his holy throne.

I lift your holy name over each of these nations, O Lord. You are worthy to be praised among all peoples of the earth, and I pray that you would be exalted over every country on this list.

TODAY'S NATIONS...

1.	Canary Islands	(Pop. 2,100,000)	% of Christians: 1.01%
2.	Morocco	(Pop. 33,000,000)	% of Christians: 0.03%
3.	Algeria	(Pop. 38,800,000)	% of Christians: 1.40%
4.	Tunisia	(Pop. 11,000,000)	% of Christians: 0.1%
5.	Libya	(Pop. 6,200,000)	% of Christians: 0.31%
6.	Egypt	(Pop. 86,900,000)	% of Christians: 3.45%
7.	Malta	(Pop. 400,000)	% of Christians: 1.39%
8.	Gibraltar	(Pop. 30,000)	% of Christians: 3.295%

Pray for the peace of Jerusalem—Psalm 122:6.

MY ADDITIONAL PERSONAL FOCUSES
(Include your own prayer list.)

_____
_____
_____
_____
_____
_____
_____
_____
_____
_____
_____
_____
_____
_____
_____
_____
_____
_____
_____
_____

9. DAY NINE

TODAY'S WATCHMAN FOCUS:

CHILDREN

(Children in Danger, Child Trafficking, and Orphans)

Jesus loved children. In Matthew 19:14 He said, "Let the little children come to me, and do not hinder them, for the kingdom of heaven belongs to such as these" (NIV). Today we remember these innocent ones of society, the children of the world. In numerous nations a vast percentage of the population is under 18 years of age, and the majority of these are under the age of 14. Some are referring to this demographic as the "4/14 Window" because most of these are in this specific age bracket. These are the most vulnerable. In some parts of Africa the adult populations of entire villages have been decimated by HIV/AIDS, leaving villages full of orphans. Child prostitution and the trafficking of young children are rampant in many nations, even in the Western world. In some parts of the world street children number in the millions and represent an unreached people group. Children need our prayers today. Pray by name for children, grandchildren, nieces, and nephews in your family. Extend your prayers to children in your neighborhood, your state, the nation, and around the world. Pray that Christian parents will raise their children to know and love the Lord. Pray for Christ-centered alternatives in TV programs, movies, video games, and music that help build a child's faith, rather than destroy it. And pray for international evangelistic programs that help share the Gospel and make disciples of children around the world.

TODAY'S PROMISE-PASSAGES

Matthew 18:2-5

Then Jesus called a little child to Him, set him in the midst of them, and said, "Assuredly, I say to you, unless you are converted and become as little children, you will by no means enter the kingdom of heaven...

Father, I pray that people all over the world would see you and your kingdom in the faces of children. I ask that ministries and churches in all nations would recognize the value of learning from and ministering to children...

...Therefore whoever humbles himself as this little child is the greatest in the kingdom of heaven. Whoever receives one little child like this in My name receives Me.

...I pray, Lord, that you would help me humble my heart and come before you with the faith and gentleness of a child. Father, give your Church your heart for children all over the world.

Matthew 19:13-15

Then little children were brought to Him that He might put *His* hands on them and pray, but the disciples rebuked them...

O Lord, I lift before you ministries around the world—specifically some I know by name—that bring children to you and care for them in your name. Bless them, Lord; help them meet physical and spiritual needs...

...But Jesus said, "Let the little children come to Me, and do not forbid them; for of such is the kingdom of heaven." And He laid *His* hands on them and departed from there.

...I pray that you would be with children in all nations today, especially those who are abandoned, orphaned, destitute, or abused. Care for them and comfort them in your Fatherly love. Protect them because they are your children, and draw them near to you.

Deuteronomy 6:6-9

"And these words which I command you today shall be in your heart. You shall teach them diligently to your children, and shall talk of them when you sit in your house, when you walk by the way, when you lie down, and when you rise up...

Lord, I bring before you families all over the world. I pray that families would raise their children to walk in your ways, that children would grow up knowing your Word and your heart, and that parents would teach their children to recognize and obey your voice...

...You shall bind them as a sign on your hand, and they shall be as frontlets between your eyes. You shall write them on the doorposts of your house and on your gates."

...I pray, Father, for homes to be filled with the knowledge and things of you. Let children grow up in environments saturated in your presence, knowing that you are the true God.

Deuteronomy 4:7-10

"For what great nation *is there* that has God so near to it, as the Lord our God *is* to us, for whatever *reason* we may call upon Him? And what great nation *is there* that has *such* statutes and righteous judgments as are in all this law which I set before you this day?...

I thank you, O Lord, that you are always with us and that we can call on you at any time, trusting that you will hear. You are a good and just God, unlike any other, and I praise you for your unfailing faithfulness to your people!

...Only take heed to yourself, and diligently keep yourself, lest you forget the things your eyes have seen, and lest they depart from your heart all the days of your life. And teach them to your children and your grandchildren...

Father, keep your will and your ways at the front of my mind and heart. I pray that parents, teachers, and all those who work with children around the world (especially the ones I know by name) would consistently speak the knowledge of who you are into the lives of those children...

...*especially concerning* the day you stood before the Lord your God in Horeb, when the Lord said to me, 'Gather the people to Me, and I will let them hear My words, that they may learn to fear Me all the days they live on the earth, and *that* they may teach their children.'"

...I ask that children would learn to serve you all the days of their lives, and that they would experience a relationship with you so that they might never wander from your paths.

PRAY GOD'S WORD OVER THE SEVEN SPHERES OF INFLUENCE:

1. **Religion**
   (The Church, Ministries, and Other Faiths)

2. **Family and Marriages**
   (Youth, Children, and the Sanctity of Marriage)

3. **Education**
   (All Schools, Universities, and Colleges)

4. **Business**
   (The Marketplace)

5. **Government**
   (Locally, Nationally, and Internationally)

6. **Media**
   (The Press, Television, Internet, and Social Networking)

7. **Arts and Entertainment**
   (Including Sports)

PRAY THE "FOUR CLAIMS" OVER TODAY'S NATIONS

1. Claim... **Open Doors**   (Colossians 4:2-3).
2. Claim... **Open Minds**   (Acts 26:17b-18a).
3. Claim... **Open Hearts**   (2 Corinthians 4:6).
4. Claim... **Open Heavens**   (Isaiah 45:8).

Note: Visit www.EHC.org for real-time prayer requests from the front lines of world evangelism.

TODAY'S PROMISE FOR THE NATIONS

Psalm 72:17-19 (NIV)

May his name endure forever; may it continue as long as the sun. All nations will be blessed through him, and they will call him blessed...

O Lord, I pray that you would establish godly leaders in all of the nations on my list today. Let these nations experience your blessing because their authorities are following your ways...

...Praise be to the LORD God, the God of Israel, who alone does marvelous deeds. Praise be to his glorious name forever; may the whole earth be filled with his glory. Amen and Amen.

...There is no other god like you, Lord, and I declare your powerful name and your glory over each of these nations today! Let the peoples praise you in all corners of these seven countries.

TODAY'S NATIONS...

1.	Portugal	(Pop. 10,800,000)	% of Christians: 3.22%
2.	Spain	(Pop. 47,700,000)	% of Christians: 1.01%
3.	Andorra	(Pop. 90,000)	% of Christians: 0.42%
4.	Switzerland	(Pop. 8,100,000)	% of Christians: 3.77%
5.	Monaco	(Pop. 30,000)	% of Christians: 1.11%
6.	Liechtenstein	(Pop. 40,000)	% of Christians: 0.5%
7.	Italy	(Pop. 61,700,000)	% of Christians: 1.13%

Pray for the peace of Jerusalem—Psalm 122:6.

MY ADDITIONAL PERSONAL FOCUSES
(Include your own prayer list.)

10. DAY TEN

TODAY'S WATCHMAN FOCUS:

JUSTICE

(The Courts and Judges of Our Nation and the Nations of the World)

Justice is defined as "the upholding of what is just, especially fair treatment in accordance with honor, standards, or law." It is to "treat adequately, fairly, or with full appreciation." The judicial branch of many governments is clearly one of the most influential of all aspects of authority. Their decisions touch the life of every citizen and, when functioning properly, help protect individuals from exploitation, settle disputes, and punish criminals who break the law. In many parts of the world, however, such justice is hardly the norm. Judges and politicians are too often corrupt, and the result is injustice at all levels of society. Today we make this a matter of our fervent prayers. Ask the Holy Spirit to show you areas in your own nation or community where justice is desperately needed. Pray specifically for nations or areas of the world that you know to be lacking in administering true justice to people, especially those nations that oppress women, minorities, Christians or the poor in general. As followers of Jesus we should be model citizens who, "Defend the poor and fatherless; do justice to the afflicted and needy. Deliver the poor and needy; free them from the hand of the wicked" (Psalm 82:3-4). Pray that God will raise up more Christian judges and lawyers locally and globally who are guided by honesty and truth.

DAY 10

TODAY'S PROMISE-PASSAGES

Proverbs 2:1-9

My son, if you receive my words, and treasure my commands within you, so that you incline your ear to wisdom, *and* apply your heart to understanding; yes, if you cry out for discernment, *and* lift up your voice for understanding, if you seek her as silver, and search for her as *for* hidden treasures...

Father, the courts and judges in my nation and in nations around the world are in desperate need of your wisdom and truth. I pray that you would create in them hearts that are receptive to your Word. Give them discernment and make them attentive to your voice and commands...

...Then you will understand the fear of the LORD, and find the knowledge of God...

...I ask, Lord, that the fear of you that is the beginning of all wisdom would fall on all those who are involved in making decisions that define justice in the nations...

...For the LORD gives wisdom; from His mouth *come* knowledge and understanding; He stores up sound wisdom for the upright; *He is* a shield to those who walk uprightly...

Increase the influence and the knowledge of those who walk in your ways, O Lord. Pour out your blessing where you find justice on the earth...

...He guards the paths of justice, and preserves the way of His saints. Then you will understand righteousness and justice, equity *and* every good path.

...Protect leaders in judicial systems who walk according to your law and make your paths clear to them. Father, establish justice through your people.

Deuteronomy 16:18-20

"You shall appoint judges and officers in all your gates, which the Lord your God gives you, according to your tribes, and they shall judge the people with just judgment...

...You shall not pervert justice; you shall not show partiality, nor take a bribe, for a bribe blinds the eyes of the wise and twists the words of the righteous...

...You shall follow what is altogether just, that you may live and inherit the land which the Lord your God is giving you."

I pray that you would establish judges and leaders in judicial systems according to your will. Guide those who elect and appoint those leaders to make godly decisions.

I pray, O Lord, that you would frustrate the plans of the wicked and make way for justice across the earth. May corruption come to an end and truth always come to light...

...And I pray for fairness, for concern for the poor who are close to your heart, and for honesty at all levels. Bring blessing on the peoples who walk in your righteousness, Father.

PRAY GOD'S WORD OVER THE SEVEN SPHERES OF INFLUENCE:

1. **Religion**
   (The Church, Ministries, and Other Faiths)

2. **Family and Marriages**
   (Youth, Children, and the Sanctity of Marriage)

3. **Education**
   (All Schools, Universities, and Colleges)

4. **Business**
   (The Marketplace)

5. **Government**
   (Locally, Nationally, and Internationally)

6. **Media**
   (The Press, Television, Internet, and Social Networking)

7. **Arts and Entertainment**
   (Including Sports)

PRAY THE "FOUR CLAIMS" OVER TODAY'S NATIONS

1. Claim... **Open Doors**   (Colossians 4:2-3).
2. Claim... **Open Minds**   (Acts 26:17b-18a).
3. Claim... **Open Hearts**   (2 Corinthians 4:6).
4. Claim... **Open Heavens**   (Isaiah 45:8).

Note: Visit www.EHC.org for real-time prayer requests from the front lines of world evangelism.

TODAY'S PROMISE FOR THE NATIONS

Isaiah 51:4-5 (NIV)

"Listen to me, my people; hear me, my nation: Instruction will go out from me; my justice will become a light to the nations...

...My righteousness draws near speedily, my salvation is on the way, and my arm will bring justice to the nations. The islands will look to me and wait in hope for my arm."

Lord, I pray that the peoples of these seven nations would live according to your ways, walking in the light of your law...

...Send your salvation swiftly, Father, to those who look to you for hope and follow your decrees in these nations. I declare your justice and righteousness over these nations today.

TODAY'S NATIONS...

1.	Vatican City	(Pop. 842)	% of Christians: not available
2.	San Marino	(Pop. 30,000)	% of Christians: < 0.1%
3.	Slovenia	(Pop. 2,000,000)	% of Christians: 0.13%
4.	Croatia	(Pop. 4,500,000)	% of Christians: 0.38%
5.	Bosnia/Herzegovina	(Pop. 3,900,000)	% of Christians: 0.22%
6.	Serbia	(Pop. 7,200,000)	% of Christians: 0.73%
7.	Kosovo	(Pop. 1,900,000)	% of Christians: 0.29%

Pray for the peace of Jerusalem—Psalm 122:6.

MY ADDITIONAL PERSONAL FOCUSES
(Include your own prayer list.)

_____
_____
_____
_____
_____
_____
_____
_____
_____
_____
_____
_____
_____
_____
_____
_____
_____
_____
_____
_____
_____

11. DAY ELEVEN

TODAY'S WATCHMAN FOCUS:

CHRISTIAN LABORERS

(Remembering Pastors, Evangelists, Teachers and Other Christian Workers)

Today our primary focus for prayer as watchmen are those who help spread or teach the Good News of Christ in our community, nation, and the nations of the world. Be specific as you pray for those you know "by name" who are serving in advancing the kingdom of Christ throughout the world. Some may be prominent leaders in the Church, known worldwide, while others may only be known to a small community of believers, including you. They need your prayers. Pray for those you know who may be beyond your theological sphere or denomination. Compile your personal list in the space provided that follows of those you want to pray for at least once each month. Some who minister specifically to you or in your community should be added to each daily list. Pray also for more laborers to be called into the harvest (Matthew 9:37-38). Pray also for those who do proclaim the Gospel, that it will be "the pure Gospel" and that all Christian workers, whether missionaries or indigenous pastors and evangelists will remember Peter's compelling words: "Nor is there salvation in any other, for there is no other name under heaven given among men by which we must be saved" (Acts 4:12).

TODAY'S PROMISE-PASSAGES

Matthew 9:35-38

Then Jesus went about all the cities and villages, teaching in their synagogues, preaching the gospel of the kingdom, and healing every sickness and every disease among the people...

Lord, in your earthly life you demonstrated the way to care for people and minister to them in the heart and name of God. I praise you for your love and power!

...But when He saw the multitudes, He was moved with compassion for them, because they were weary and scattered, like sheep having no shepherd...

But my heart breaks with yours, Father, as I see people who are lost in darkness without you. I ask that you would give me your compassion as I see the faces of those who so desperately need guidance to find you...

...Then He said to His disciples, "The harvest truly *is* plentiful, but the laborers *are* few. Therefore pray the Lord of the harvest to send out laborers into His harvest."

...Father, so many people are ready to find you but need someone to show them the way. So I pray that you would raise up and send your servants to lead and shepherd your people.

Romans 10:13-15

For "whoever calls on the name of the LORD shall be saved."...

I praise you, O Lord, for your salvation. Thank you that you save all those who call on your name!

...How then shall they call on Him in whom they have not believed? And how shall they believe in Him of whom they have not heard? And how shall they hear without a preacher?...

Father, I lift the lost in my nation and around the world before you. I especially pray for people groups who have never heard the Gospel before...

...And how shall they preach unless they are sent? As it is written: "How beautiful are the feet of those who preach the gospel of peace, Who bring glad tidings of good things!"

...I pray that you would send your servants to these people—servants who would share the truth of the Gospel. I pray that all those whom you call would go where you send them. Speak to my heart, Father, about who you would have me share the Gospel with.

Hebrews 13:17-18

Obey those who rule over you, and be submissive, for they watch out for your souls, as those who must give account. Let them do so with joy and not with grief, for that would be unprofitable for you...

Father, I pray that the leaders you place over your people would remain faithful to your call and will, becoming channels of your love and grace who shepherd your people just as you would...

...Pray for us; for we are confident that we have a good conscience, in all things desiring to live honorably.

...I lift up those laborers I know by name and pray that you would keep them near your heart. Give them your wisdom, O Lord, and reveal yourself to your people through them.

1 Thessalonians 5:12-18

And we urge you, brethren, to recognize those who labor among you, and are over you in the Lord and admonish you, and to esteem them very highly in love for their work's sake. Be at peace among yourselves...

Father, I bring before you those who are laboring for your kingdom today. I thank you that they answered your call, and I pray that you would make their work fruitful. I ask that unity in your Spirit would come before all else so that your servants in all churches, denominations, and ministries would work together in peace for your glory.

...Now we exhort you, brethren, warn those who are unruly, comfort the fainthearted, uphold the weak, be patient with all. See that no one renders evil for evil to anyone, but always pursue what is good both for yourselves and for all...

I pray, O Lord, that as Christian laborers spread your Gospel, it would be pure and true. I pray that you would give these laborers your heart and empower them to minister to your people as you would...

...Rejoice always, pray without ceasing, in everything give thanks; for this is the will of God in Christ Jesus for you.

...Give your laborers a heart of praise, a commitment to prayer, and a spirit of thanksgiving, Lord. As they labor, let these things be poured into the hearts of those they lead to you.

PRAY GOD'S WORD OVER THE SEVEN SPHERES OF INFLUENCE:

1. **Religion**
   (The Church, Ministries, and Other Faiths)

2. **Family and Marriages**
   (Youth, Children, and the Sanctity of Marriage)

3. **Education**
   (All Schools, Universities, and Colleges)

4. **Business**
   (The Marketplace)

5. **Government**
   (Locally, Nationally, and Internationally)

6. **Media**
   (The Press, Television, Internet, and Social Networking)

7. **Arts and Entertainment**
   (Including Sports)

PRAY THE "FOUR CLAIMS" OVER TODAY'S NATIONS

1. Claim... **Open Doors** (Colossians 4:2-3).
2. Claim... **Open Minds** (Acts 26:17b-18a).
3. Claim... **Open Hearts** (2 Corinthians 4:6).
4. Claim... **Open Heavens** (Isaiah 45:8).

Note: Visit www.EHC.org for real-time prayer requests from the front lines of world evangelism.

TODAY'S PROMISE FOR THE NATIONS

Psalm 86:9-10 (NIV)

All the nations you have made will come and worship before you, Lord; they will bring glory to your name...

Father, you are the creator of all things and worthy to be praised in all nations on earth! I pray that all the nations on my list today would come to worship you for the glory of your name...

...For you are great and do marvelous deeds; you alone are God.

...I declare your greatness over these nations and ask that you would make your wonderful works known among these peoples, O Lord.

TODAY'S NATIONS...

1.	Montenegro	(Pop. 700,000)	% of Christians: 0.14%
2.	Macedonia	(Pop. 2,100,000)	% of Christians: 0.24%
3.	Albania	(Pop. 3,000,000)	% of Christians: 0.40%
4.	Greece	(Pop. 10,800,000)	% of Christians: 0.54%
5.	Bulgaria	(Pop. 6,900,000)	% of Christians: 1.80%
6.	Romania	(Pop. 21,700,000)	% of Christians: 5.10%
7.	Hungary	(Pop. 9,900,000)	% of Christians: 2.75%

Pray for the peace of Jerusalem—Psalm 122:6.

MY ADDITIONAL PERSONAL FOCUSES
(Include your own prayer list.)

12. DAY TWELVE

TODAY'S WATCHMAN FOCUS:

THE POOR AND SUFFERING

(Praying for the Issue of Global Poverty and Hunger)

DAY 12

God's Word and Christ's sacrifice for all mankind compel us to show compassion to the poor and suffering. As you thank the Lord today for the provision of food to eat and good health, focus your specific prayers on those who have very little to eat and those who suffer in poverty. This primary focus for today embodies all those who may live in constant pain resulting from sickness or malnutrition. Use the passages of Scripture selected for today to pray for these precious people who not only need the basics of life just to live but who also need the message of salvation in Christ so they might inherit eternal life. Think especially of those living in impoverished parts of the world where there seems to be almost perpetual famine and suffering. Multiplied millions live in constant hunger every day which often results in a variety of sicknesses that otherwise would be prevented with proper nourishment.

TODAY'S PROMISE-PASSAGES

Isaiah 58:6-11

Is this not the fast that I have chosen: To loose the bonds of wickedness, To undo the heavy burdens, to let the oppressed go free, and that you break every yoke?...

Lord, I know you have not called your people to perform religious rituals or to fast for our own purposes, for these things are not glorifying to you. Rather, you call us to worship you by caring for your people...

...*Is it* not to share your bread with the hungry, and that you bring to your house the poor who are cast out; when you see the naked, that you cover him, and not hide yourself from your own flesh?...

...*Therefore I pray, Father, that your Church across the earth would take on your burden for those who are suffering from sickness, poverty, disease, and malnutrition both inside and outside of your family...*

...Then your light shall break forth like the morning, your healing shall spring forth speedily, and your righteousness shall go before you; the glory of the LORD shall be your rear guard. Then you shall call, and the LORD will answer; you shall cry, and He will say, 'Here I *am*.' "If you take away the yoke from your midst, The pointing of the finger, and speaking wickedness...

Lord, teach us to seek you in caring for one another and to find you in meeting needs. Let us be an extension of your love for your people. Let us walk in your righteousness by caring for the afflicted, and surround us with your light and glory as we do so. Purify and unify us as your people as we learn to reflect you in seeking the good of those around us...

...*If* you extend your soul to the hungry and satisfy the afflicted soul, then your light shall dawn in the darkness, and your darkness shall *be* as the noonday...

...*Father, I thank you for the ways you have provided for me, and I pray you would open my eyes to the needs of your people and show me how to give myself to them...*

...The LORD will guide you continually, and satisfy your soul in drought, and strengthen your bones; you shall be like a watered garden, and like a spring of water whose waters do not fail.

I praise you, O Lord, that you give guidance and strength to us as we seek to become like you in providing for the poor and suffering who are so close to your heart.

Psalm 22:26-28

"The poor shall eat and be satisfied; those who seek Him will praise the LORD. Let your heart live forever...

I pray, Father, that you would satisfy the longings of the poor, giving them strength to praise you. Give your heart to the suffering as you deliver them...

...All the ends of the world shall remember and turn to the LORD, and all the families of the nations shall worship before You. For the kingdom *is* the LORD's, and He rules over the nations."

...I pray that in every nation, your people would remember and worship you for all the ways you provide in times of poverty and distress. You are Lord over all circumstances, and I pray that the nations would remember this and worship you in all times.

Isaiah 41:17-20

"The poor and needy seek water, but *there is* none, their tongues fail for thirst. I, the LORD, will hear them; I, the God of Israel, will not forsake them...

Father, I lift the poor and suffering in all corners of the world to you today. I pray that you would remember them and rescue them from sickness and poverty...

...I will open rivers in desolate heights, and fountains in the midst of the valleys; I will make the wilderness a pool of water, and the dry land springs of water. I will plant in the wilderness the cedar and the acacia tree, the myrtle and the oil tree; I will set in the desert the cypress tree *and* the pine and the box tree together...

...I pray, O Lord, that you would send not only material provision, but also the waters of eternal life. Satisfy the needy with the everlasting life of your salvation and with the physical resources they need to live today. Let life spring up even where death once seemed certain.

...That they may see and know, and consider and understand together, that the hand of the LORD has done this, and the Holy One of Israel has created it."

I ask this, Father, for the sake of the glory of your name. Reveal yourself as you provide so that all nations might see you and worship you.

Psalm 12:5

"For the oppression of the poor, for the sighing of the needy, now I will arise," says the LORD; "I will set *him* in the safety for which he yearns."

O Lord, I pray that you would arise and move on behalf of the poor and suffering. Meet their needs and bring them into your haven of safety.

PRAY GOD'S WORD OVER
THE SEVEN SPHERES OF INFLUENCE:

1. Religion
   (The Church, Ministries, and Other Faiths)

2. Family and Marriages
   (Youth, Children, and the Sanctity of Marriage)

3. Education
   (All Schools, Universities, and Colleges)

4. Business
   (The Marketplace)

5. Government
   (Locally, Nationally, and Internationally)

6. Media
   (The Press, Television, Internet, and Social Networking)

7. Arts and Entertainment
   (Including Sports)

PRAY THE "FOUR CLAIMS" OVER
TODAY'S NATIONS

1. Claim... **Open Doors** (Colossians 4:2-3).
2. Claim... **Open Minds** (Acts 26:17b-18a).
3. Claim... **Open Hearts** (2 Corinthians 4:6).
4. Claim... **Open Heavens** (Isaiah 45:8).

Note: Visit www.EHC.org for real-time prayer requests from the front lines of world evangelism.

TODAY'S PROMISE FOR THE NATIONS

Psalm 96:3-4 (NIV)

Declare his glory among the nations, his marvelous deeds among all peoples. For great is the LORD and most worthy of praise; he is to be feared above all gods.

Lord, I declare your glory and might over these nations today. I pray that the knowledge of who you are and what you have done would be made known, and that the fear of the Lord would fill these lands. You are great and worthy of such praise!

TODAY'S NATIONS...

1.	Austria	(Pop. 8,200,000)	% of Christians: 0.48%
2.	Slovakia	(Pop. 5,400,000)	% of Christians: 1.26%
3.	Czech Republic	(Pop. 10,600,000)	% of Christians: 0.74%
4.	Germany	(Pop. 81,000,000)	% of Christians: 2.07%
5.	Poland	(Pop. 38,300,000)	% of Christians: 0.34%
6.	Denmark	(Pop. 5,600,000)	% of Christians: 3.77%
7.	Netherlands	(Pop. 16,900,000)	% of Christians: 4.15%

Pray for the peace of Jerusalem—Psalm 122:6.

MY ADDITIONAL PERSONAL FOCUSES
(Include your own prayer list.)

_____

_____

_____

_____

_____

_____

_____

_____

_____

_____

_____

_____

_____

_____

_____

_____

_____

_____

_____

_____

13. DAY THIRTEEN

TODAY'S WATCHMAN FOCUS:

THE DISABLED

(Those Developmentally Impaired and the Handicapped)

Daily life is difficult for people who were born with physical or mental challenges or who were left disabled by a severe illness or injury. Often some of the most neglected people in many parts of the world are those with serious handicaps or various physical or mental impairments. They also can be the most severely mistreated and regularly abused. Today, in addition to all else we claim in prayer as watchmen, we especially weep over these, praying that God will touch followers of Jesus in these areas to seek out the needs of such people and to find ways to love and care for them—in the name of Jesus. Prayerfully remember those in this condition in distant places on our planet as well as those who live in your community. Do some "prayer homework" and learn of ministries that specifically target the disabled and pray for them as well as support them in their mandate to care for and disciple the disabled. Pray also for the creation of more church-based outreaches to the disabled in local communities. Pray that every church, especially in the underdeveloped regions of the world, will be sensitive to the needs of the disabled who are part of their congregation or people they know. Pray by name for disabled people you may know at church or in your neighborhood or village. Also pray for family members and caregivers who help loved ones with special needs.

DAY 13

TODAY'S PROMISE-PASSAGES

Job 29:12-16

Because I delivered the poor who cried out, the fatherless and *the one who* had no helper. The blessing of a perishing *man* came upon me, and I caused the widow's heart to sing for joy...

Father, I know that you care for those who are disabled, and yet they are so often neglected or abused. I pray that you would turn the hearts of your servants in all nations toward these people groups...

...I put on righteousness, and it clothed me; my justice *was* like a robe and a turban. I was eyes to the blind, and I was feet to the lame...

...Teach us to treat the disabled with respect and to fight for justice on their behalf. Remind us to provide for them because they are your children...

...I *was* a father to the poor, and I searched out the case *that* I did not know.

...Make our hearts sensitive to the needs of those who are disabled, and show us how we can reveal Jesus to them.

Isaiah 35:4-7

Say to those *who are* fearful-hearted, "Be strong, do not fear! Behold, your God will come *with* vengeance, *with* the recompense of God; He will come and save you."...

O Lord, I pray that you would be near the hearts of those who are disabled. Comfort them and assure them of your presence and your salvation...

...Then the eyes of the blind shall be opened, and the ears of the deaf shall be unstopped. Then the lame shall leap like a deer, and the tongue of the dumb sing...

...I ask, Father, for healing from disabilities—both for those who were born with impairments and for those who have been disabled from injuries. You are able to heal, and I ask that you would. I pray specifically for those with disabilities I know by name...

...For waters shall burst forth in the wilderness, and streams in the desert. The parched ground shall become a pool, and the thirsty land springs of water; in the habitation of jackals, where each lay, *there shall be* grass with reeds and rushes.

...I pray that you would pour out your life and provision on all those who have disabilities, Lord. Bless those ministries who care for them, and empower more churches and ministries to do the same.

Zephaniah 3:17-20

"The LORD your God in your midst, the Mighty One, will save; He will rejoice over you with gladness, He will quiet *you* with His love, He will rejoice over you with singing." "I will gather those who sorrow over the appointed assembly, who are among you, *to whom* its reproach *is* a burden...

...Behold, at that time I will deal with all who afflict you; I will save the lame, and gather those who were driven out; I will appoint them for praise and fame in every land where they were put to shame...

...At that time I will bring you back, even at the time I gather you; for I will give you fame and praise among all the peoples of the earth, when I return your captives before your eyes," says the LORD.

Father, I pray that you would give your peace and joy to those who are disabled. Let them understand how precious they are in your sight. Let your Church communicate the worth of every individual through love—and through love in action, extending your care to those who need it...

...O Lord, protect your children who are disabled from those who would wish to harm or take advantage of them. Raise up your servants to defend their lives and livelihoods, and bless those ministries that do so already.

I pray for restoration, Father, for bodies, minds, and all forms of health. Bring your people together as one Body, including those who are disabled, and let our love for one another and value of every individual be a witness of your love to the world.

PRAY GOD'S WORD OVER THE SEVEN SPHERES OF INFLUENCE:

1. **Religion**
   (The Church, Ministries, and Other Faiths)

2. **Family and Marriages**
   (Youth, Children, and the Sanctity of Marriage)

3. **Education**
   (All Schools, Universities, and Colleges)

4. **Business**
   (The Marketplace)

5. **Government**
   (Locally, Nationally, and Internationally)

6. **Media**
   (The Press, Television, Internet, and Social Networking)

7. **Arts and Entertainment**
   (Including Sports)

PRAY THE "FOUR CLAIMS" OVER TODAY'S NATIONS

1. Claim... **Open Doors** (Colossians 4:2-3).
2. Claim... **Open Minds** (Acts 26:17b-18a).
3. Claim... **Open Hearts** (2 Corinthians 4:6).
4. Claim... **Open Heavens** (Isaiah 45:8).

Note: Visit www.EHC.org for real-time prayer requests from the front lines of world evangelism.

TODAY'S PROMISE FOR THE NATIONS

Psalm 96:7-9 (NIV)

Ascribe to the LORD, all you families of nations, ascribe to the LORD glory and strength. Ascribe to the LORD the glory due his name...

Today, I declare over the nations on my list your power, and I pray that all peoples in these nations would see and exalt you...

...bring an offering and come into his courts. Worship the LORD in the splendor of his holiness; tremble before him, all the earth.

...May all the peoples of these nations give their lives as an offering to you and worship you as you deserve, O Lord!

TODAY'S NATIONS...

1.	Belgium	(Pop. 10,400,000)	% of Christians: 1.27%
2.	Luxembourg	(Pop. 500,000)	% of Christians: 0.68%
3.	France	(Pop. 66,300,000)	% of Christians: 1.02%
4.	Channel Islands	(Pop. 200,000)	% of Christians: 8.08%
5.	Ireland	(Pop. 4,800,000)	% of Christians: 1.38%
6.	United Kingdom	(Pop. 63,700,000)	% of Christians: 8.08%
7.	Faroe Islands	(Pop. 50,000)	% of Christians: 28.10%

Pray for the peace of Jerusalem—Psalm 122:6.

MY ADDITIONAL PERSONAL FOCUSES
(Include your own prayer list.)

14. DAY FOURTEEN

TODAY'S WATCHMAN FOCUS:

PRISONERS

(The Incarcerated)

"I was in prison and you came to visit me" (Matthew 25:36, NIV). Thousands of prison inmates who have lost their freedom and are separated from their families long to find forgiveness that only Christ can offer. Although many might not view people incarcerated as an unreached people group, many millions of men and women globally are in prisons, jails, and under house arrest and thus dwell outside the stream of much of today's conventional evangelism and discipleship outreaches. Today our primary focus for prayer touches those in this category of people who need the Good News of Jesus. Because many of these are long-term prisoners, we need to pray for strategies that seek to minister to these people right where they live and even provide means to help those who come to Christ in prisons to plant churches in these institutions that are self-sustaining. Pray not only for prisoners to come to Christ while incarcerated but for prison ministries to cultivate ongoing contact with these new believers so they will mature in their faith. Pray also for prisoners who do come to Christ that when paroled they will find fellowship with strong believers who will help them grow in Jesus and make a meaningful contribution to society. The families of inmates also need to experience a special sense of God's love and guidance while their loved ones are in prison. Pray that God will provide special comfort for the spouses, children, and relatives of prison inmates and that any prisoners incarcerated unjustly will be set free.

TODAY'S PROMISE-PASSAGES

Hebrews 13:1-3

Let brotherly love continue. Do not forget to entertain strangers, for by so *doing* some have unwittingly entertained angels...

Father, I pray that you would remind us, as your people, to treat everyone with an abundance of love and respect—for we know that you alone judge our hearts...

...Remember the prisoners as if chained with them—those who are mistreated—since you yourselves are in the body also.

...Teach us to reach out to those who are in prison, remembering that we have all sinned and are offered a second chance to live in the righteousness of Christ.

Psalm 69:30-34

I will praise the name of God with a song, and will magnify Him with thanksgiving...

Father, I pray for those prisoners who have come to worship you as they serve their sentences. I praise you that they have found you and recognize your glory!

...*This* also shall please the LORD better than an ox *or* bull, which has horns and hooves. The humble shall see *this and* be glad; and you who seek God, your hearts shall live...

Restore those who are experiencing new life in you, O Lord. Transform them in your likeness and let their hope be a witness to their fellow prisoners and prison staff. Revive their hearts and keep them close to you. Give them fellowship with other believers...

...For the LORD hears the poor, and does not despise His prisoners. Let heaven and earth praise Him, the seas and everything that moves in them.

...Thank you, Father, that you care for and desire the salvation of every prisoner around the world. I pray that each prisoner who finds you would be changed forever.

Psalm 146:5-7

Happy *is* he who *has* the God of Jacob for his help, whose hope *is* in the Lord his God, who made heaven and earth, the sea, and all that *is* in them; who keeps truth forever...

You are a good and faithful God, and I thank you that I am blessed to place my hope in you. I pray that you would help us share your hope with those who are in prison...

...Who executes justice for the oppressed, who gives food to the hungry. The Lord gives freedom to the prisoners.

...And because you are a God of justice, I ask that you would free any prisoners around the world who might be unjustly incarcerated.

PRAY GOD'S WORD OVER
THE SEVEN SPHERES OF INFLUENCE:

1. Religion
   (The Church, Ministries, and Other Faiths)

2. Family and Marriages
   (Youth, Children, and the Sanctity of Marriage)

3. Education
   (All Schools, Universities, and Colleges)

4. Business
   (The Marketplace)

5. Government
   (Locally, Nationally, and Internationally)

6. Media
   (The Press, Television, Internet, and Social Networking)

7. Arts and Entertainment
   (Including Sports)

PRAY THE "FOUR CLAIMS" OVER
TODAY'S NATIONS

1. Claim... **Open Doors**   (Colossians 4:2-3).
2. Claim... **Open Minds**   (Acts 26:17b-18a).
3. Claim... **Open Hearts**   (2 Corinthians 4:6).
4. Claim... **Open Heavens**   (Isaiah 45:8).

Note: Visit www.EHC.org for real-time prayer requests from the front lines of world evangelism.

TODAY'S PROMISE FOR THE NATIONS

Psalm 106:47 (NIV)

Save us, LORD our God, and gather us from the nations, that we may give thanks to your holy name and glory in your praise.

O Lord, I declare your salvation over these eight nations today! Let the peoples of each one bring thanksgiving and honor to you.

TODAY'S NATIONS...

	Nation	Population	% of Christians
1.	Norway	(Pop. 5,100,000)	% of Christians: 8.49%
2.	Sweden	(Pop. 9,700,000)	% of Christians: 6.53%
3.	Finland	(Pop. 5,300,000)	% of Christians: 11.91%
4.	Estonia	(Pop. 1,300,000)	% of Christians: 4.41%
5.	Latvia	(Pop. 2,200,000)	% of Christians: 5.34%
6.	Lithuania	(Pop. 3,500,000)	% of Christians: 1.07%
7.	Belarus	(Pop. 9,600,000)	% of Christians: 1.31%
8.	Ukraine	(Pop. 44,300,000)	% of Christians: 3.23%

Pray for the peace of Jerusalem—Psalm 122:6.

MY ADDITIONAL PERSONAL FOCUSES
(Include your own prayer list.)

_____

_____

_____

_____

_____

_____

_____

_____

_____

_____

_____

_____

_____

_____

_____

_____

_____

_____

_____

15. DAY FIFTEEN

TODAY'S WATCHMAN FOCUS:

GLOBAL EVANGELISM AND DISCIPLESHIP

(Ministries, Denominations, and Mission Agencies Committed to Gathering in and Discipling the Great End-Time Harvest)

The mission of the Church is called the Great Commission—to faithfully carry out Christ's command to "go...and make disciples of all the nations" (Matthew 28:19). It's a two-pronged strategy of sharing the Gospel with the lost to help lead them to faith in Jesus Christ and then discipling new believers through sound Bible teaching in order to preserve fruit that remains (John 15:16). In addition to all that we might pray for today as we fulfill our assignment as watchmen on our Wall of Prayer, we specifically want to focus on today's primary theme—worldwide movements, denominations, strategies, and ministries committed to global evangelism and discipleship. Jesus commissioned His disciples to go and disciple the nations, "teaching them to observe all" that He commanded them (Matthew 28:19-20). Most believers are familiar with key ministries, denominations, and other agencies with a vision to reach the lost and disciple them. Many of these are involved in church planting. Pray for those ministries you know "by name" that specifically seek to share the Good News of Jesus everywhere and disciple those who respond and desire to know Christ as Savior.

DAY 15

TODAY'S PROMISE-PASSAGES

Matthew 24:14

And this gospel of the kingdom will be preached in all the world as a witness to all the nations, and then the end will come.

Father, I pray that your Gospel would go forth in all nations so that every person in all corners of the earth would have the opportunity to hear the name of Jesus.

Matthew 28:18-20

And Jesus came and spoke to them, saying, "All authority has been given to Me in heaven and on earth...

Thank you, Lord, that you have equipped your Church with your authority and the power of your name to take the Gospel to the world...

...Go therefore and make disciples of all the nations, baptizing them in the name of the Father and of the Son and of the Holy Spirit...

...I pray over ministries that focus on global evangelism—particularly those I know by name. Make their labor fruitful. Give existing ministries wisdom and strategy, and raise up new ministries with innovative, biblically-grounded visions for evangelism...

...teaching them to observe all things that I have commanded you; and lo, I am with you always, *even* to the end of the age." Amen.

...Father, sustain the harvests of global evangelism with effective discipleship that would transform new believers into the likeness of Christ. Thank you that you are with your Church wherever your Gospel is taken!

John 4:34-38

Jesus said to them, "My food is to do the will of Him who sent Me, and to finish His work...

Father, make us like your Son so that our hearts might find satisfaction in doing the work of your will...

...Do you not say, 'There are still four months and *then* comes the harvest'? Behold, I say to you, lift up your eyes and look at the fields, for they are already white for harvest...

...Open our eyes to the work that you have set before us. I thank you that your Spirit prepares the hearts and minds of the lost so that they might hear your truth in the Gospel...

...And he who reaps receives wages, and gathers fruit for eternal life, that both he who sows and he who reaps may rejoice together...

Thank you, O Lord, that thousands of people are finding you every day! I pray that you would continue to send your Spirit before the efforts of evangelism...

...For in this the saying is true: 'One sows and another reaps.' I sent you to reap that for which you have not labored; others have labored, and you have entered into their labors."

...And I ask for unity among ministries and missions organizations as they work for the same purpose for you. Let them share in one heart and vision as they seek the salvation and discipleship of all nations.

PRAY GOD'S WORD OVER THE SEVEN SPHERES OF INFLUENCE:

1. **Religion**
   (The Church, Ministries, and Other Faiths)

2. **Family and Marriages**
   (Youth, Children, and the Sanctity of Marriage)

3. **Education**
   (All Schools, Universities, and Colleges)

4. **Business**
   (The Marketplace)

5. **Government**
   (Locally, Nationally, and Internationally)

6. **Media**
   (The Press, Television, Internet, and Social Networking)

7. **Arts and Entertainment**
   (Including Sports)

PRAY THE "FOUR CLAIMS" OVER TODAY'S NATIONS

1. Claim... **Open Doors**   (Colossians 4:2-3).
2. Claim... **Open Minds**   (Acts 26:17b-18a).
3. Claim... **Open Hearts**   (2 Corinthians 4:6).
4. Claim... **Open Heavens**   (Isaiah 45:8).

Note: Visit www.EHC.org for real-time prayer requests from the front lines of world evangelism.

TODAY'S PROMISE FOR THE NATIONS

Psalm 98:1-2 (NIV)

Sing to the LORD a new song, for he has done marvelous things; his right hand and his holy arm have worked salvation for him...

I praise you, O Lord, for your wonderful deeds! I declare your victory over the nations on my list today...

...The LORD has made his salvation known and revealed his righteousness to the nations.

...Let salvation spread throughout these lands as the peoples look upon your holiness, Father.

TODAY'S NATIONS...

1.	Moldova	(Pop. 3,600,000)	% of Christians: 3.56%
2.	Georgia	(Pop. 4,600,000)	% of Christians: 1.33%
3.	Armenia	(Pop. 3,100,000)	% of Christians: 8.55%
4.	Azerbaijan	(Pop. 9,700,000)	% of Christians: 0.22%
5.	Russia	(Pop. 142,500,000)	% of Christians: 1.22%
6.	Kazakhstan	(Pop. 17,900,000)	% of Christians: 0.63%
7.	Uzbekistan	(Pop. 28,900,000)	% of Christians: 0.22%

Pray for the peace of Jerusalem—Psalm 122:6.

MY ADDITIONAL PERSONAL FOCUSES
(Include your own prayer list.)

_____
_____
_____
_____
_____
_____
_____
_____
_____
_____
_____
_____
_____
_____
_____
_____
_____
_____
_____
_____
_____

16. DAY SIXTEEN

TODAY'S WATCHMAN FOCUS:

OTHER FAITHS AND BELIEF SYSTEMS

Millions of people embrace belief systems and ideologies that claim to point the way to salvation through some system of self-sacrifice and good works yet miss the transforming power of the cross and resurrection. The Apostle Paul taught that "if anyone is in Christ, he is a new creation; the old has gone, the new has come!" (2 Corinthians 5:17, NIV). Pray that believers in all nations will have opportunities to share the reality of knowing Christ with those who have never experienced His "amazing grace." Especially pray for the various faiths of the world, as well as the many organizations and individuals focused on demonstrating the compassion of Christ among people of these groups. Pray that the growing "prayer, care, share" strategy of truly praying for and loving those of other faiths through caring for and helping meet their felt needs will become a global strategy of the Body of Christ. Pray "by name" for neighbors and friends you know who embrace different belief systems, asking God to enable you to share the Good News of your own testimony with them in love and humility.

TODAY'S PROMISE-PASSAGES

Acts 17:24-31

"God, who made the world and everything in it, since He is Lord of heaven and earth, does not dwell in temples made with hands. Nor is He worshiped with men's hands, as though He needed anything, since He gives to all life, breath, and all things...

I praise you, O Lord, for there is none like you. No other god is the creator, giver, and sustainer of all life as you are. You have no need of the work of our hands for the sake of your existence or our salvation...

...And He has made from one blood every nation of men to dwell on all the face of the earth, and has determined their preappointed times and the boundaries of their dwellings...

...You are Lord over all the earth, orchestrating all the details of the times and seasons of life, and our desire is that all people would worship you.

...so that they should seek the Lord, in the hope that they might grope for Him and find Him, though He is not far from each one of us; for in Him we live and move and have our being, as also some of your own poets have said, 'For we are also His offspring.'...

I pray, Father, for those who are lost in the darkness of other faiths and belief systems. Foster within them a dissatisfaction that would lead them to seek you. Reveal yourself to them in your grace and make the gospel message clear to their hearts so that they might desire your everlasting life...

...Therefore, since we are the offspring of God, we ought not to think that the Divine Nature is like gold or silver or stone, something shaped by art and man's devising...

...Open the eyes of those who worship idols to see the emptiness and lifelessness of that which they serve. Show yourself as the living God who is the divine Father of the nations...

...Truly, these times of ignorance God overlooked, but now commands all men everywhere to repent, because He has appointed a day on which He will judge the world in righteousness by the Man whom He has ordained. He has given assurance of this to all by raising Him from the dead."

...Thank you, O Lord, for your complete forgiveness and offer of salvation. I pray that those of other faiths and belief systems would be attracted to your mercy and grace and would surrender their lives to you.

Acts 3:19-21

Repent therefore and be converted, that your sins may be blotted out, so that times of refreshing may come from the presence of the Lord...

O Lord, I lift those of other faiths to you and ask that you would turn hearts away from false beliefs and toward you for salvation and restoration...

...and that He may send Jesus Christ, who was preached to you before, whom heaven must receive until the times of restoration of all things, which God has spoken by the mouth of all His holy prophets since the world began.

...I pray that they would hear the story of the life and work of Jesus and accept His sacrifice for their redemption, entering into the new life of His resurrection. Let them accept Jesus as the only way to you, the one true God.

Acts 26:16-18

"But rise and stand on your feet; for I have appeared to you for this purpose, to make you a minister and a witness both of the things which you have seen and of the things which I will yet reveal to you. I will deliver you from the *Jewish* people, as well as *from the Gentiles,* to whom I now send you...

Father, I pray that you would prepare and appoint passionate witnesses to people groups of other faiths and belief systems. Let them be courageous and give them wisdom to interact with specific worldviews. You know how to reach the hearts of these peoples, and I pray that you would equip your servants with that understanding...

...to open their eyes, *in order* to turn *them* from darkness to light, and *from* the power of Satan to God, that they may receive forgiveness of sins and an inheritance among those who are sanctified by faith in Me."

...And I ask that as people of other belief systems come to find you, they would become bold and effective witnesses among their own faith communities. Let their testimonies carry power and bring many more into your kingdom, O Lord.

PRAY GOD'S WORD OVER
THE SEVEN SPHERES OF INFLUENCE:

1. Religion
   (The Church, Ministries, and Other Faiths)

2. Family and Marriages
   (Youth, Children, and the Sanctity of Marriage)

3. Education
   (All Schools, Universities, and Colleges)

4. Business
   (The Marketplace)

5. Government
   (Locally, Nationally, and Internationally)

6. Media
   (The Press, Television, Internet, and Social Networking)

7. Arts and Entertainment
   (Including Sports)

PRAY THE "FOUR CLAIMS" OVER
TODAY'S NATIONS

1. Claim... **Open Doors** (Colossians 4:2-3).
2. Claim... **Open Minds** (Acts 26:17b-18a).
3. Claim... **Open Hearts** (2 Corinthians 4:6).
4. Claim... **Open Heavens** (Isaiah 45:8).

Note: Visit www.EHC.org for real-time prayer requests from the front lines of world evangelism.

TODAY'S PROMISE FOR THE NATIONS

Psalm 99:1-2 (NIV)

The LORD reigns, let the nations tremble; he sits enthroned between the cherubim, let the earth shake...

Father, I pray that the peoples of these eight nations would tremble before you today. Let them see your power and authority...

...Great is the LORD in Zion; he is exalted over all the nations.

...I exalt your name over each nation here and declare that you are Lord above all.

TODAY'S NATIONS...

1.	Turkmenistan	(Pop. 5,200,000)	% of Christians: < 0.1%
2.	Kyrgyzstan	(Pop. 5,600,000)	% of Christians: 0.41%
3.	Tajikistan	(Pop. 8,100,000)	% of Christians: 0.14%
4.	Turkey	(Pop. 81,600,000)	% of Christians: < 0.1%
5.	Cyprus	(Pop. 1,200,000)	% of Christians: 1.15%
6.	Lebanon	(Pop. 5,900,000)	% of Christians: 0.59%
7.	Syria	(Pop. 18,000,000)	% of Christians: 0.15%
8.	Israel	(Pop. 7,800,000)	% of Christians: 0.23%

Pray for the peace of Jerusalem—Psalm 122:6.

MY ADDITIONAL PERSONAL FOCUSES
(Include your own prayer list.)

_____

_____

_____

_____

_____

_____

_____

_____

_____

_____

_____

_____

_____

_____

_____

_____

_____

_____

_____

17. DAY SEVENTEEN

TODAY'S WATCHMAN FOCUS:

UNREACHED PEOPLES

A compelling love for the lost led Jesus to the cross to die for the sins of the world, yet nearly 2,000 years later millions of inhabitants live among unreached people groups that have yet to receive a clear presentation of the Gospel. Pray that geographical, political, and other barriers that hinder the spread of the Gospel to these people groups will be overcome. Pray that God will divinely call and save key individuals from every people group to help share the Good News, make disciples, and plant churches among all people groups and nations. Pray for ministries using Christian radio programs, gospel literature, and recorded gospel messages to help introduce these many unreached people groups to Christ. Pray especially for growing movements focusing on evangelism and discipleship for non-readers (the illiterate), increasingly referred to as "oral learners." Draw encouragement from the apostle John's vision in heaven: "After these things I looked, and behold, a great multitude which no one could number, of all nations, tribes, peoples and tongues, standing before the throne and before the Lamb, clothed in white robes, with palm branches in their hands" (Revelation 7:9).

TODAY'S PROMISE-PASSAGES

Revelation 7:9-12

After these things I looked, and behold, a great multitude which no one could number, of all nations, tribes, peoples, and tongues, standing before the throne and before the Lamb, clothed with white robes, with palm branches in their hands...

Today I come before you, Lord, on behalf of unreached people groups around the world. I desire to see the reality of this vision—the salvation of all tribes and tongues on earth. You are worthy to be worshiped by the multitudes of the world's distant lands...

...and crying out with a loud voice, saying, "Salvation *belongs* to our God who sits on the throne, and to the Lamb!"...

Father, I pray that you would send messengers of your salvation to the uttermost parts of the world where the Gospel has not yet been preached...

...All the angels stood around the throne and the elders and the four living creatures, and fell on their faces before the throne and worshiped God, saying: "Amen! Blessing and glory and wisdom, thanksgiving and honor and power and might, *be* to our God forever and ever. Amen."

...Draw all peoples to your throne, O Lord, and let them see your glory. Open their eyes in the darkness to see your light. We know you desire the salvation and reverence of all humanity, and so I pray that all unreached people groups would be reached for the honor of your name.

Romans 15:20-21

And so I have made it my aim to preach the gospel, not where Christ was named, lest I should build on another man's foundation...

Father, I pray that you would help your Church identify unreached people groups and call your servants to take the Gospel to them...

...but as it is written: "To whom He was not announced, they shall see; And those who have not heard shall understand."

...Let those who go to unreached people groups find innovative and effective means of sharing the Gospel, especially among those who are oral learners or who have unique dialects or languages.

John 10:15-16

As the Father knows Me, even so I know the Father; and I lay down My life for the sheep...

I thank you, Father, that you sent your Son to die for every person on earth, and I pray for those who have not heard this Good News yet...

...And other sheep I have which are not of this fold; them also I must bring, and they will hear My voice; and there will be one flock *and* one shepherd.

...I ask that you would break down all barriers—whether political, social, geographical, or other—that would prevent those precious souls from hearing of you, and send forth your Gospel swiftly into those unreached lands.

PRAY GOD'S WORD OVER
THE SEVEN SPHERES OF INFLUENCE:

1. Religion
   (The Church, Ministries, and Other Faiths)

2. Family and Marriages
   (Youth, Children, and the Sanctity of Marriage)

3. Education
   (All Schools, Universities, and Colleges)

4. Business
   (The Marketplace)

5. Government
   (Locally, Nationally, and Internationally)

6. Media
   (The Press, Television, Internet, and Social Networking)

7. Arts and Entertainment
   (Including Sports)

PRAY THE "FOUR CLAIMS" OVER
TODAY'S NATIONS

1. Claim... **Open Doors** (Colossians 4:2-3).
2. Claim... **Open Minds** (Acts 26:17b-18a).
3. Claim... **Open Hearts** (2 Corinthians 4:6).
4. Claim... **Open Heavens** (Isaiah 45:8).

Note: Visit www.EHC.org for real-time prayer requests from the front lines of world evangelism.

TODAY'S PROMISE FOR THE NATIONS

Psalm 102:15 (NIV)

The nations will fear the name of the LORD, all the kings of the earth will revere your glory.

O Lord, spread a reverence for you across these nations I am lifting up in prayer today. Let the leaders of these nations fall before you in worship and submit themselves and their countries to you.

TODAY'S NATIONS...

1.	Kuwait	(Pop. 2,700,000)	% of Christians: 1.27%
2.	Iraq	(Pop. 32,600,000)	% of Christians: 0.29%
3.	Jordan	(Pop. 7,900,000)	% of Christians: 0.27%
4.	Saudi Arabia	(Pop. 27,300,000)	% of Christians: 0.55%
5.	Bahrain	(Pop. 1,300,000)	% of Christians: 2.43%
6.	United Arab Emirates	(Pop. 5,600,000)	% of Christians: 1.39%
7.	Yemen	(Pop. 26,100,000)	% of Christians: < 0.1%

Pray for the peace of Jerusalem—Psalm 122:6.

MY ADDITIONAL PERSONAL FOCUSES
(Include your own prayer list.)

_____

_____

_____

_____

_____

_____

_____

_____

_____

_____

_____

_____

_____

_____

_____

_____

_____

_____

_____

_____

_____

_____

18. DAY EIGHTEEN

TODAY'S WATCHMAN FOCUS:

LIBERTY AND FREEDOM

(Issues of Human Rights and Individual Freedoms)

One of the most important of the "seven spheres of influence" involves government and politics. People around the world are willing to lay down their lives for the freedoms expressed in the United States' Declaration of Independence in 1776: "We hold these truths to be self-evident, that all men are created equal, that they are endowed by their Creator with certain unalienable Rights, that among these are Life, Liberty and the pursuit of Happiness." Pray that none of us who live in nations with such freedoms will ever forget that liberty and freedom are gifts from God that can be lost if we turn our backs on Him. No matter what levels of freedom you may have where you live, pray that God will intervene in your national and local governments in ways that promote individual freedoms. Especially remember in prayer those people in parts of the world (particularly in the Middle East) undergoing significant democratic reforms with the hopes of promoting and securing more personal freedoms. In nations with free elections, pray that more devoted, righteous people will seek and be elected to public office, thus helping provide a moral compass for their communities and nations, for where there is no vision, the people perish (Proverbs 28:18).

TODAY'S PROMISE-PASSAGES

Isaiah 61:1-7

"The Spirit of the Lord Gḷ *is* upon Me, because the LḷṚḅ has anointed Me to preach good tidings to the poor; He has sent Me to heal the brokenhearted, to proclaim liberty to the captives, and the opening of the prison to *those who are* bound; to proclaim the acceptable year of the LḷṚḅ, and the day of vengeance of our God; to comfort all who mourn...

...To console those who mourn in Zion, to give them beauty for ashes, the oil of joy for mourning, the garment of praise for the spirit of heaviness; that they may be called trees of righteousness, the planting of the LḷṚḅ, that He may be glorified."...

...And they shall rebuild the old ruins, they shall raise up the former desolations, and they shall repair the ruined cities, the desolations of many generations. Strangers shall stand and feed your flocks, and the sons of the foreigner *shall be* your plowmen and your vinedressers...

...But you shall be named the priests of the LḷṚḅ, they shall call you the servants of our God. You shall eat the riches of the Gentiles, and in their glory you shall boast...

...Instead of your shame *you shall have* double *honor,* and *instead of* confusion they shall rejoice in their portion. Therefore in their land they shall possess double; everlasting joy shall be theirs."

O Father, I pray that you would extend your hand across the nations today in favor of freedom. I lift up those who are living in nations of captivity, stripped of basic liberties—would you shake those nations so that freedom might be established. I also pray for those who live in freedom, that you would establish righteousness and moral leaders among them...

...I pray especially, Lord, for those countries I know are in turmoil as their peoples seek to establish or reestablish freedom. Direct those peoples and lead the authorities of those nations so that oppression might cease and liberty go forth instead...

Bless those nations where freedom is protected and used wisely, Father. Where freedom is newly found, I pray that you would lend your hand to stabilize those lands you lift out of oppression. Bless the people and renew the nations where liberty is pursued and individual rights are defended...

...I pray, Lord, that as freedom spreads, so would knowledge of you. Let those who walk in freedom share their faith boldly as steadfast ministers of the Gospel...

...Open new doors of freedom in closed nations so that your Word might go forth unhindered. Let freedom fall on all the earth for the sake of your name, and let that freedom testify to who you are and how you created the earth.

Romans 8:19-21

For the earnest expectation of the creation eagerly waits for the revealing of the sons of God. For the creation was subjected to futility, not willingly, but because of Him who subjected *it* in hope...

Father, we know that you intended all of creation to live in your freedom. That freedom was compromised by sin and death, but you began restoring such liberty with the arrival of your kingdom in the life of Jesus...

...because the creation itself also will be delivered from the bondage of corruption into the glorious liberty of the children of God.

...I pray, Lord, that you would free your creation according to your will, bringing liberty to the captives and releasing the land from its anxious longings.

PRAY GOD'S WORD OVER THE SEVEN SPHERES OF INFLUENCE:

1. Religion
   (The Church, Ministries, and Other Faiths)

2. Family and Marriages
   (Youth, Children, and the Sanctity of Marriage)

3. Education
   (All Schools, Universities, and Colleges)

4. Business
   (The Marketplace)

5. Government
   (Locally, Nationally, and Internationally)

6. Media
   (The Press, Television, Internet, and Social Networking)

7. Arts and Entertainment
   (Including Sports)

PRAY THE "FOUR CLAIMS" OVER TODAY'S NATIONS

1. Claim... **Open Doors** (Colossians 4:2-3).
2. Claim... **Open Minds** (Acts 26:17b-18a).
3. Claim... **Open Hearts** (2 Corinthians 4:6).
4. Claim... **Open Heavens** (Isaiah 45:8).

Note: Visit www.EHC.org for real-time prayer requests from the front lines of world evangelism.

TODAY'S PROMISE FOR THE NATIONS

Psalm 105:1-2 (NIV)

Give thanks to the LORD, proclaim his name; make known among the nations what he has done. Sing to him, sing praise to him; tell of all his wonderful acts.

O Lord, I pray that all peoples in these seven nations would know of your mighty works. Let them praise you as they see and experience your goodness and strength.

TODAY'S NATIONS...

1.	Oman	(Pop. 3,200,000)	% of Christians: 0.74%
2.	Qatar	(Pop. 2,100,000)	% of Christians: 1.0%
3.	Iran	(Pop. 80,800,000)	% of Christians: 0.39%
4.	Afghanistan	(Pop. 31,800,000)	% of Christians: 0.05%
5.	Pakistan	(Pop. 196,200,000)	% of Christians: 0.75%
6.	India	(Pop. 1,236,300,000)	% of Christians: 2.17%
7.	Maldive Islands	(Pop. 400,000)	% of Christians: 0.10%

Pray for the peace of Jerusalem—Psalm 122:6.

MY ADDITIONAL PERSONAL FOCUSES
(Include your own prayer list.)

_____

_____

_____

_____

_____

_____

_____

_____

_____

_____

_____

_____

_____

_____

_____

_____

_____

_____

19. DAY NINETEEN

TODAY'S WATCHMAN FOCUS:

AIDS, MALARIA, AND PANDEMIC DISEASES

Diseases in the developing world often strike without warning, affecting thousands of people. More than a million people die from malaria every day. Since 1981 the global HIV/AIDS epidemic has spread into all sectors of society, killing more than 30 million people and infecting another 34 million with the HIV virus. Pray for dedicated medical missionaries who treat the sick in remote mission hospitals around the world. Pray for health workers involved in disease prevention and education programs. Pray that Christians will have opportunities to share the Gospel with the sick and dying and lead the lost to Christ, the One who "heals the brokenhearted and binds up their wounds" (Psalm 147:3).

DAY 19

TODAY'S PROMISE-PASSAGES

Isaiah 53:3-5

He is despised and rejected by men, a Man of sorrows and acquainted with grief. And we hid, as it were, *our* faces from Him; He was despised, and we did not esteem Him...

I thank you, O Lord, that you bore our sicknesses in your death, paying the price for our healing. You took the penalty of sin on yourself so that we might have the fullest life...

...Surely He has borne our griefs and carried our sorrows; yet we esteemed Him stricken, smitten by God, and afflicted...

...I pray for workers who serve those who are afflicted with pandemic diseases like you did, Lord, giving their lives for the sake of caring for others. Let there be opportunity for them to share your love as well as physical treatment...

...But He *was* wounded for our transgressions, *He was* bruised for our iniquities; the chastisement for our peace *was* upon Him, and by His stripes we are healed.

...Prepare and send more of your servants, Father, who would be medical missionaries and share the hope of your Gospel with those who are sick and dying from HIV/AIDS, malaria, and other pandemic diseases.

Psalm 103:1-6

Bless the LORD, O my soul; and all that is within me, *bless* His holy name! Bless the LORD, O my soul, and forget not all His benefits...

...Who forgives all your iniquities, who heals all your diseases, who redeems your life from destruction, who crowns you with loving kindness and tender mercies...

...Who satisfies your mouth with good *things, so that* your youth is renewed like the eagle's. The LORD executes righteousness and justice for all who are oppressed.

I praise you, O Lord, for you are a faithful God who is able to heal. We know that you are Lord over all sickness and disease...

Today I lift before you all those who are afflicted with pandemic diseases like HIV/AIDS and malaria, especially in countries where treatment is poor or limited...

...I ask for healing, Father. I pray that treatments would be effective and that access to them would increase. Slow the spread of these diseases and help us improve preventative measures.

PRAY GOD'S WORD OVER THE SEVEN SPHERES OF INFLUENCE:

1. Religion
   (The Church, Ministries, and Other Faiths)

2. Family and Marriages
   (Youth, Children, and the Sanctity of Marriage)

3. Education
   (All Schools, Universities, and Colleges)

4. Business
   (The Marketplace)

5. Government
   (Locally, Nationally, and Internationally)

6. Media
   (The Press, Television, Internet, and Social Networking)

7. Arts and Entertainment
   (Including Sports)

PRAY THE "FOUR CLAIMS" OVER TODAY'S NATIONS

1. Claim... **Open Doors** (Colossians 4:2-3).
2. Claim... **Open Minds** (Acts 26:17b-18a).
3. Claim... **Open Hearts** (2 Corinthians 4:6).
4. Claim... **Open Heavens** (Isaiah 45:8).

Note: Visit www.EHC.org for real-time prayer requests from the front lines of world evangelism.

TODAY'S PROMISE FOR THE NATIONS

Psalm 96:10-11 (NIV)

Say among the nations, "The LORD reigns." The world is firmly established, it cannot be moved; he will judge the peoples with equity. Let the heavens rejoice, let the earth be glad; let the sea resound, and all that is in it.

Father, I declare your reign over the nations on my list today. Let them see you and know that you are Lord above all. I pray that these nations would rejoice in you and praise you for your greatness.

TODAY'S NATIONS...

1.	Sri Lanka	(Pop. 21,900,000)	% of Christians: 2.02%
2.	Bangladesh	(Pop. 166,300,000)	% of Christians: 0.37%
3.	Nepal	(Pop. 31,000,000)	% of Christians: .59%
4.	Bhutan	(Pop. 700,000)	% of Christians: .74%
5.	Myanmar	(Pop. 55,700,000)	% of Christians: 5.12%
6.	Thailand	(Pop. 67,700,000)	% of Christians: 0.49%
7.	Laos	(Pop. 6,800,000)	% of Christians: 1.84%

Pray for the peace of Jerusalem—Psalm 122:6.

MY ADDITIONAL PERSONAL FOCUSES
(Include your own prayer list.)

20. DAY TWENTY

TODAY'S WATCHMAN FOCUS:

CIVIL SERVANTS

(Police, Firefighters, and Others Who Serve in Our Communities)

Men and women who hold city, state, or federal jobs serve within one of the "seven spheres of influence" that are foundational to government structures around the world. The responsibilities they have and the decisions they make impact communities on multiple levels and in ways that may affect thousands of people. Pray that public servants will act responsibly in their jobs. Pray "by name" for people you may know who work in the public sector. Also pray that Christians will stand out as model employees as they mirror Christ's example of a faithful servant, mindful of His words: "If anyone desires to be first, he shall be last of all and servant of all" (Mark 9:35). Pray especially for the police of your community that they will be protected as they often go into harm's way. Pray against all corruption that can often be tempting to those in such positions of trust. Pray, too, for the families of those in law enforcement, as often the intensity of their work impacts their home life in negative ways. The same is true for firefighters who generally have to live away from home for many days at a time in order to be on call at all hours of the day and night.

DAY 20

TODAY'S PROMISE-PASSAGES

Philippians 2:1-10

Therefore if *there is* any consolation in Christ, if any comfort of love, if any fellowship of the Spirit, if any affection and mercy, fulfill my joy by being like-minded, having the same love, *being* of one accord, of one mind...

I thank you, Father, for the privilege of knowing you and being part of your family. Today I pray on behalf of civil servants who work in various levels of public service offices and operations, especially those in my country...

...*Let* nothing *be done* through selfish ambition or conceit, but in lowliness of mind let each esteem others better than himself. Let each of you look out not only for his own interests, but also for the interests of others...

...I thank you for the work they do, and I pray that their hearts would be sensitive to the people and communities they serve so that they would place the interests of others before their own. I pray specifically for those I know by name...

...Let this mind be in you which was also in Christ Jesus, who, being in the form of God, did not consider it robbery to be equal with God, but made Himself of no reputation, taking the form of a bondservant, *and* coming in the likeness of men...

As Christ so humbly came to the earth to serve the world, I pray that these workers would humbly perform their jobs in service to the people. Give them wisdom as they make decisions and perform tasks that affect their communities...

...And being found in appearance as a man, He humbled Himself and became obedient to *the point of* death, even the death of the cross...

...Protect those who place themselves in the line of danger for the sake of their communities, Father. Keep them and their families secure in you, and give them discernment and strength when they encounter perilous situations...

...Therefore God also has highly exalted Him and given Him the name which is above every name, that at the name of Jesus every knee should bow, of those in heaven, and of those on earth, and of those under the earth...

...I pray that through the work of these civil servants in public affairs, you would be glorified. Let the name of Jesus be lifted high in my nation through the example of those who serve our communities.

Galatians 5:13-15

For you, brethren, have been called to liberty; only do not *use* liberty as an opportunity for the flesh, but through love serve one another...

...For all the law is fulfilled in one word, even in this: *"You shall love your neighbor as yourself."*...

...But if you bite and devour one another, beware lest you be consumed by one another!

Father, we are grateful for civil servants who choose to dedicate their lives to the work of caring for their communities. I pray especially for Christian workers in these fields...

...Give them opportunities to speak of your love as they serve others. I pray that they would always stand for what is right...

...Keep the hands of all civil servants from corruption and pour out your blessing on them as they serve and care for others.

PRAY GOD'S WORD OVER
THE SEVEN SPHERES OF INFLUENCE:

1. Religion
   (The Church, Ministries, and Other Faiths)

2. Family and Marriages
   (Youth, Children, and the Sanctity of Marriage)

3. Education
   (All Schools, Universities, and Colleges)

4. Business
   (The Marketplace)

5. Government
   (Locally, Nationally, and Internationally)

6. Media
   (The Press, Television, Internet, and Social Networking)

7. Arts and Entertainment
   (Including Sports)

PRAY THE "FOUR CLAIMS" OVER
TODAY'S NATIONS

1. Claim... **Open Doors** (Colossians 4:2-3).

2. Claim... **Open Minds** (Acts 26:17b-18a).

3. Claim... **Open Hearts** (2 Corinthians 4:6).

4. Claim... **Open Heavens** (Isaiah 45:8).

Note: Visit www.EHC.org for real-time prayer requests from the front lines of world evangelism.

TODAY'S PROMISE FOR THE NATIONS

Psalm 108:3-5 (NIV)

I will praise you, LORD, among the nations; I will sing of you among the peoples...

Lord, I praise your name and give you thanks for all that you have done! Let the nations see you and bring you thanks...

...For great is your love, higher than the heavens; your faithfulness reaches to the skies. Be exalted, O God, above the heavens, and let your glory be over all the earth.

...Today I pray that your truth would go forth in these eight nations. Make your unfailing love known among these peoples. I exalt you and your glory over these nations today, O Lord!

TODAY'S NATIONS...

1.	Cambodia	(Pop. 15,500,000)	% of Christians: 1.67%
2.	Vietnam	(Pop. 93,400,000)	% of Christians: 1.76%
3.	Malaysia	(Pop. 30,100,000)	% of Christians: 3.20%
4.	Singapore	(Pop. 5,600,000)	% of Christians: 6.14%
5.	Brunei	(Pop. 400,000)	% of Christians: 5.22%
6.	Indonesia	(Pop. 253,600,000)	% of Christians: 2.78%
7.	East Timor	(Pop. 1,200,000)	% of Christians: 2.24%
8.	Seychelles	(Pop. 90,000)	% of Christians: 5.90%

Pray for the peace of Jerusalem—Psalm 122:6.

MY ADDITIONAL PERSONAL FOCUSES
(Include your own prayer list.)

_____

_____

_____

_____

_____

_____

_____

_____

_____

_____

_____

_____

_____

_____

_____

_____

_____

_____

_____

_____

21. DAY TWENTY-ONE

TODAY'S WATCHMAN FOCUS:

HUMANITARIAN MINISTRIES

(Charities, Non-Profit Agencies, and NGOs)

Christian humanitarian ministries, often referred to in foreign nations as NGOs or "Non-Government Organizations," provide aid to people living in extreme poverty or who have become victims of natural disasters, wars, and other unexpected tragedies. They see Christ in those they serve, remembering His words in Matthew 25:35: "For I was hungry, and you gave Me food; I was thirsty and you gave Me drink; I was a stranger and you took Me in." Pray "by name" for humanitarian ministries you support or are familiar with and add them to today's prayer list. Pray for the protection of Christian aid workers who often travel into dangerous war zones and unstable areas to minister to people in need. Especially pray that Christian ministries will not compromise their responsibility to share the Gospel with the people they minister to. Pray they will have many opportunities to share the message of salvation openly in areas that might not otherwise be freely open to Christian evangelism.

TODAY'S PROMISE-PASSAGES

Luke 10:30-37

Then Jesus answered and said: "A certain *man* went down from Jerusalem to Jericho, and fell among thieves, who stripped him of his clothing, wounded *him*, and departed, leaving *him* half dead...

Father, today I lift up organizations that serve those in need of humanitarian aid—charities, non-profits, and NGOs around the world. Thank you that such groups exist to do this work of caring for the physical needs of your children...

...Now by chance a certain priest came down that road. And when he saw him, he passed by on the other side. Likewise a Levite, when he arrived at the place, came and looked, and passed by on the other side...

So many people in so many countries are in need of basic necessities and care, and I thank you that so many ministries exist to ensure that they are not overlooked. Give these ministries eyes to see the true needs of the people they serve...

...But a certain Samaritan, as he journeyed, came where he was. And when he saw him, he had compassion...

...Give your heart of compassion and grace to these humanitarian ministries, Lord, and give them opportunities to speak of your love...

...So he went to *him* and bandaged his wounds, pouring on oil and wine; and he set him on his own animal, brought him to an inn, and took care of him. On the next day, when he departed, he took out two denarii, gave *them* to the innkeeper, and said to him, 'Take care of him; and whatever more you spend, when I come again, I will repay you.'...

Bless these ministries with strategies and resources, Father. I pray that they would have the workers and volunteers they need and the means to meet the needs they encounter. Give them wisdom and discernment to make decisions that benefit those they serve. Help them understand cultural and social dynamics when they work in foreign nations...

...So which of these three do you think was neighbor to him who fell among the thieves?" And he said, "He who showed mercy on him." Then Jesus said to him, "Go and do likewise."

...And Lord, let the Gospel go forth in the work of these groups. As they meet physical needs, help them identify and meet spiritual needs. Let them mirror you in everything they do.

Matthew 25:32-36

"All the nations will be gathered before Him, and He will separate them one from another, as a shepherd divides *his* sheep from the goats. And He will set the sheep on His right hand, but the goats on the left...

I pray, Father, over all the volunteers and workers of humanitarian ministries. Guard them as they travel into war-torn and poverty-stricken areas. I pray specifically for ministries and people I know by name. Protect them so that they can care for others...

Then the King will say to those on His right hand, 'Come, you blessed of My Father, inherit the kingdom prepared for you from the foundation of the world...

I pray that the work of these humanitarian ministries would be pure and saturated by the Gospel. Let all work done in your name be glorifying and pleasing to you...

...for I was hungry and you gave Me food; I was thirsty and you gave Me drink; I was a stranger and you took Me in; I *was* naked and you clothed Me; I was sick and you visited Me; I was in prison and you came to Me.'"

...Lord, help those laboring with these ministries to see you in the faces of the people they care for. Thank you for allowing us to encounter you in our relationships with others, Father, and help us treat people with the love and respect you desire.

Proverbs 3:27-29

Do not withhold good from those to whom it is due, when it is in the power of your hand to do so...

I ask, Lord, for an abundance of resources for humanitarian ministries. I pray that they would be able to meet the needs they encounter...

...Do not say to your neighbor, "Go, and come back, and tomorrow I will give it," when you have it with you...

....Keep these ministries faithful as they use the resources you entrust to them. I also ask for unique opportunities to share the Gospel where it might otherwise have been prohibited...

...Do not devise evil against your neighbor, for he dwells by you for safety's sake.

...Let your love pour through these humanitarian workers so that the impoverished and unstable areas in which they work might be completely transformed for your glory.

PRAY GOD'S WORD OVER
THE SEVEN SPHERES OF INFLUENCE:

1. Religion
   (The Church, Ministries, and Other Faiths)

2. Family and Marriages
   (Youth, Children, and the Sanctity of Marriage)

3. Education
   (All Schools, Universities, and Colleges)

4. Business
   (The Marketplace)

5. Government
   (Locally, Nationally, and Internationally)

6. Media
   (The Press, Television, Internet, and Social Networking)

7. Arts and Entertainment
   (Including Sports)

PRAY THE "FOUR CLAIMS" OVER
TODAY'S NATIONS

1. Claim... **Open Doors** (Colossians 4:2-3).
2. Claim... **Open Minds** (Acts 26:17b-18a).
3. Claim... **Open Hearts** (2 Corinthians 4:6).
4. Claim... **Open Heavens** (Isaiah 45:8).

Note: Visit www.EHC.org for real-time prayer requests
from the front lines of world evangelism.

TODAY'S PROMISE FOR THE NATIONS

Psalm 113:3-5 (NIV)

From the rising of the sun to the place where it sets, the name of the LORD is to be praised...

...The LORD is exalted over all the nations, his glory above the heavens. Who is like the LORD our God, the One who sits enthroned on high.

O Lord, I ask that prayer and worship would arise to you from these seven nations day and night...

...You are God over each of these nations, and there is none like you! Let the peoples of these nations see you enthroned in glory, Father.

TODAY'S NATIONS...

1.	Papua New Guinea	(Pop. 6,600,000)	% of Christians: 22.39%
2.	Australia	(Pop. 22,500,000)	% of Christians: 14.16%
3.	New Zealand	(Pop. 4,400,000)	% of Christians: 18.97%
4.	New Caledonia	(Pop. 300,000)	% of Christians: 5.45%
5.	Fiji	(Pop. 900,000)	% of Christians: 19.68%
6.	Vanuatu	(Pop. 300,000)	% of Christians: 41.01%
7.	Solomon Islands	(Pop. 600,000)	% of Christians: 31.54%

Pray for the peace of Jerusalem—Psalm 122:6.

MY ADDITIONAL PERSONAL FOCUSES
(Include your own prayer list.)

22. DAY TWENTY-TWO

TODAY'S WATCHMAN FOCUS:

YOUTH
(The Next Generation)

DAY 22

Young people, especially teenagers, are bombarded with immoral messages and temptations through movies, TV, music, and the Internet. Social networking is adding to this dilemma. We need to enter into the spiritual battle that is raging for the souls of our youth. The words of Proverbs are still true today: "Train up a child in the way he should go, and even when he is old he will not depart from it" (Proverbs 22:6). Pray "by name" for youth leaders in your church and the churches of your community. Ask God to raise up many who can meaningfully share His Word and encourage young people to follow the Lord. Pray for effective youth programs in our churches that will attract young people from our communities who need to hear the Gospel. Pray that churches will offer courses to help train Christian youth in how to share their faith with non-Christian friends.

TODAY'S PROMISE-PASSAGES

Psalm 119:9-16

How can a young man cleanse his way? By taking heed according to Your word...

Today I come to you, Father, on behalf of the youth in my nation and in nations around the world. I pray that you would cultivate in this generation a desire to surrender to you...

...With my whole heart I have sought You; oh, let me not wander from Your commandments! Your word I have hidden in my heart, that I might not sin against You...

...Teach today's youth to seek you and pursue your will. I pray for engaging and effective ministry programs that would draw youth to your heart and establish them in your Word...

...Blessed are *You*, O LORD! Teach me Your statutes. With my lips I have declared all the judgments of Your mouth. I have rejoiced in the way of Your testimonies, as *much as* in all riches...

...And I pray for people who would be willing and able to minister to youth. Let there be members of the church whose hearts are turned toward youth and who would be specially equipped to communicate and interact with a sometimes difficult-to-reach generation...

...I will meditate on Your precepts, and contemplate Your ways. I will delight myself in Your statutes; I will not forget Your word.

Father, fill today's youth with a longing for you and a hunger to live in your Word. Give them a passion to share their testimonies and the Gospel with everyone they can reach.

Proverbs 3:1-6

My son, do not forget my law, but let your heart keep my commands; for length of days and long life and peace they will add to you...

Lord, I lift up the youth and youth ministry leaders I know by name, and I pray that they would be firmly grounded in the Scriptures. Let them find rest and peace in you alone, Lord, and guard their hearts against the distractions of the world...

...Let not mercy and truth forsake you; bind them around your neck, write them on the tablet of your heart, *and* so find favor and high esteem in the sight of God and man...

...I pray over the relationships of today's youth—relationships with family, peers, authority figures, and you, Father. Give this generation a special measure of your grace and kindness so that they would experience and offer your love. Let your truth reign in their lives, Lord...

...Trust in the LORD with all your heart, and lean not on your own understanding; in all your ways acknowledge Him, and He shall direct your paths.

...I ask that today's youth would learn to rely on you, to walk in your will, and to follow your guidance at all times. Let them grow consistently in knowledge of and faith in you, and make them a light of your love.

PRAY GOD'S WORD OVER THE SEVEN SPHERES OF INFLUENCE:

1. Religion
   (The Church, Ministries, and Other Faiths)

2. Family and Marriages
   (Youth, Children, and the Sanctity of Marriage)

3. Education
   (All Schools, Universities, and Colleges)

4. Business
   (The Marketplace)

5. Government
   (Locally, Nationally, and Internationally)

6. Media
   (The Press, Television, Internet, and Social Networking)

7. Arts and Entertainment
   (Including Sports)

PRAY THE "FOUR CLAIMS" OVER TODAY'S NATIONS

1. Claim... **Open Doors** (Colossians 4:2-3).
2. Claim... **Open Minds** (Acts 26:17b-18a).
3. Claim... **Open Hearts** (2 Corinthians 4:6).
4. Claim... **Open Heavens** (Isaiah 45:8).

Note: Visit www.EHC.org for real-time prayer requests from the front lines of world evangelism.

TODAY'S PROMISE FOR THE NATIONS

Psalm 117:1-2 (NIV)

Praise the LORD, all you nations; extol him, all you peoples. For great is his love toward us, and the faithfulness of the LORD endures forever. Praise the LORD.

I declare your praise over the nations on my list today, O Lord! I pray that these nations would see your love and truth and choose to worship you for all time. Let the peoples praise your name!

TODAY'S NATIONS...

1.	Cook Islands	(Pop. 10,000)	% of Christians: 11.69%
2.	Niue	(Pop. 1,300)	% of Christians: 8.32%
3.	Pitcairn	(Pop. 48)	% of Christians: 10.0%
4.	Tonga	(Pop. 100,000)	% of Christians: 15.73%
5.	American Samoa	(Pop. 50,000)	% of Christians: 21.83%
6.	Samoa	(Pop. 200,000)	% of Christians: 18.66%
7.	Tokelau	(Pop. 1,377)	% of Christians: 3.4%
8.	Wallis & Futuna	(Pop. 20,000)	% of Christians: 1.0%

Pray for the peace of Jerusalem—Psalm 122:6.

MY ADDITIONAL PERSONAL FOCUSES
(Include your own prayer list.)

23. DAY TWENTY-THREE

TODAY'S WATCHMAN FOCUS:

SCRIPTURE ENGAGEMENT AND BIBLE TRANSLATION

(All God's Word for All the World)

"Thy Word is a lamp unto my feet, and a light unto my path" (Psalm 119:105, KJV). All followers of Jesus need to be engaged in God's Word on a daily basis for healthy spiritual maturity. A knowledge of God's Word is critical for both evangelism and discipleship. Pray for dedicated Bible translators who often spend years living among isolated people groups as they learn the language of a people and then seek to translate the Bible into their local dialects. Pray for programs and ministries that provide church leaders in least-evangelized nations with sound training in theology, biblical interpretation, and teaching. Pray for ministries and Bible societies that are dedicated to translating and producing Bibles and distributing them throughout the world. And especially pray that all believers everywhere will be drawn into God's Word on a regular basis so they may mature in their Christian walk.

DAY 23

TODAY'S PROMISE-PASSAGES

2 Timothy 3:14-17

But you must continue in the things which you have learned and been assured of, knowing from whom you have learned *them*...

Father, I pray that believers across the earth would hunger for your Word, and that those who are privileged to have the Scriptures in their languages would be diligent in studying them...

...and that from childhood you have known the Holy Scriptures, which are able to make you wise for salvation through faith which is in Christ Jesus...

...I thank you for the ministries and people who are committed to translating the Bible so that all peoples might have access to it. I pray that you would give them insight and understanding as they seek to learn languages and dialects in remote and isolated areas around the world...

...All Scripture *is* given by inspiration of God, and *is* profitable for doctrine, for reproof, for correction, for instruction in righteousness, that the man of God may be complete, thoroughly equipped for every good work.

...I thank you, Lord, that your Word is powerful, and I pray that it would go forth to all tribes and tongues. I also pray that all nations would have access to good Bible training. Equip your Church with the skills to read, understand, interpret, and apply Scripture appropriately, O Lord.

Isaiah 55:8-11

"For My thoughts *are* not your thoughts, nor *are* your ways My ways," says the LORD...

...

I praise you, Father, for your powerful and incomparable Word. Thank you for revealing yourself to us through the Scriptures. Help us understand the mysteries of you through your Word...

...

..."For *as* the heavens are higher than the earth, so are My ways higher than your ways, and My thoughts than your thoughts...

...

...Guard your Word, O Lord, as it is translated from language to language. Preserve your message so that it goes forth without error. Give wisdom to translators so that they are able to communicate concepts correctly and precisely in new languages...

...

..."For as the rain comes down, and the snow from heaven, and do not return there, but water the earth, and make it bring forth and bud, that it may give seed to the sower and bread to the eater...

...

Thank you, Father, that your Word always accomplishes what you intend. I pray that you would send your Word into new areas of unreached people groups for the sake of their salvation and the glory of your name...

...

...So shall My word be that goes forth from My mouth; it shall not return to Me void, but it shall accomplish what I please, and it shall prosper *in the thing* for which I sent it."

...

...And I pray for sound biblical training, especially in areas where there are large populations of unreached peoples. Let churches and ministries teach your Word in purity and truth.

PRAY GOD'S WORD OVER THE SEVEN SPHERES OF INFLUENCE:

1. **Religion**
   (The Church, Ministries, and Other Faiths)

2. **Family and Marriages**
   (Youth, Children, and the Sanctity of Marriage)

3. **Education**
   (All Schools, Universities, and Colleges)

4. **Business**
   (The Marketplace)

5. **Government**
   (Locally, Nationally, and Internationally)

6. **Media**
   (The Press, Television, Internet, and Social Networking)

7. **Arts and Entertainment**
   (Including Sports)

PRAY THE "FOUR CLAIMS" OVER TODAY'S NATIONS

1. Claim... **Open Doors**   (Colossians 4:2-3).
2. Claim... **Open Minds**   (Acts 26:17b-18a).
3. Claim... **Open Hearts**   (2 Corinthians 4:6).
4. Claim... **Open Heavens**   (Isaiah 45:8).

Note: Visit www.EHC.org for real-time prayer requests from the front lines of world evangelism.

TODAY'S PROMISE FOR THE NATIONS

Isaiah 5:26 (NIV)

He lifts up a banner for the distant nations, he whistles for those at the ends of the earth. Here they come, swiftly and speedily!

O Lord, I pray that you would call each of these seven nations to you so that they might serve and worship you!

TODAY'S NATIONS...

1.	Tuvalu	(Pop. 10,000)	% of Christians: 17.69%
2.	Kiribati	(Pop. 100,000)	% of Christians: 7.48%
3.	Nauru	(Pop. 9,000)	% of Christians: 11.72%
4.	Marshall Islands	(Pop. 70,000)	% of Christians: 42.28%
5.	Micronesia, Fed. States	(Pop. 100,000)	% of Christians: 22.42%
6.	Palau	(Pop. 20,000)	% of Christians: 21.94%
7.	Guam	(Pop. 200,000)	% of Christians: 14.80%

Pray for the peace of Jerusalem—Psalm 122:6.

MY ADDITIONAL PERSONAL FOCUSES
(Include your own prayer list.)

24. DAY TWENTY-FOUR

TODAY'S WATCHMAN FOCUS:
THE PERSECUTED CHURCH

Christ reminded His followers that being one of His disciples would not be easy. "If they persecuted Me, they will also persecute you," Jesus said (John 15:20). "Blessed are those who have been persecuted for the sake of righteousness, for theirs is the kingdom of heaven" (Matthew 5:10). Vast numbers of believers in certain nations are presently in prison merely for the "crime" of being a follower of Jesus or for sharing the Gospel with their neighbors and friends. Although most government officials in the free world frown on religious intolerance of any kind that leads to violence, persecution of Christians seems to be on a dramatic increase in recent years in some regions of the world. Pray for supernatural protection for believers who risk their lives to follow Christ in these difficult places. Pray that believers in such troubled lands will have the courage to continue in their pursuit of sharing the Good News as Christ commanded them, no matter the circumstances. Pray also for ministries that quietly provide resources to aid persecuted believers globally.

DAY 24

TODAY'S PROMISE-PASSAGES

Matthew 5:10-12

"Blessed *are* those who are persecuted for righteousness' sake, for theirs is the kingdom of heaven...

I pray for the persecuted Church around the world, Father, bringing before you those of the Body of Christ who are suffering for the sake of your name...

...Blessed are you when they revile and persecute you, and say all kinds of evil against you falsely for My sake...

...Lord, give those who are facing persecution an understanding of your presence with them and blessing on them as your Word describes...

...Rejoice and be exceedingly glad, for great *is* your reward in heaven, for so they persecuted the prophets who were before you."

...Give them peace and joy in the midst of such trials. Let them rejoice in your strength, and let their joy be a witness to those who persecute them.

1 Peter 4:12-16

Beloved, do not think it strange concerning the fiery trial which is to try you, as though some strange thing happened to you...

Father, we know that suffering is part of the Christian life. I pray that those who are suffering would not be surprised or confused by it...

...but rejoice to the extent that you partake of Christ's sufferings, that when His glory is revealed, you may also be glad with exceeding joy...

...Let them take comfort in the fact that they suffer with Christ. Give them joy and teach their hearts to praise you in the midst of painful circumstances...

...If you are reproached for the name of Christ, blessed *are you,* for the Spirit of glory and of God rests upon you. On their part He is blasphemed, but on your part He is glorified...

...Lord, be near to all those who are persecuted because of their witness for you. Let your Spirit rest upon them and give them peace...

...But let none of you suffer as a murderer, a thief, an evildoer, or as a busybody in other people's matters. Yet if *anyone suffers* as a Christian, let him not be ashamed, but let him glorify God in this matter.

...Comfort them and give them confidence in your presence, Father. Make them ever-aware of your nearness, and let them rest in the knowledge that you are still God in their situations.

2 Corinthians 1:8-11

For we do not want you to be ignorant, brethren, of our trouble which came to us in Asia: that we were burdened beyond measure, above strength, so that we despaired even of life...

Lord, we know that your Word tells us we will experience persecution for the sake of your name, but we thank you that it also encourages us with wisdom to face that persecution boldly...

...Yes, we had the sentence of death in ourselves, that we should not trust in ourselves but in God who raises the dead...

...This reminds us of how dependent we are on you, Father. Today I lift up the persecuted Church and ask that you would give those who are suffering grace and strength to trust you alone...

...who delivered us from so great a death, and does deliver us; in whom we trust that He will still deliver us...

...Teach them to place their hope and reliance in you. We can trust you with all of our needs, even in the midst of hardship...

...you also helping together in prayer for us, that thanks may be given by many persons on our behalf for the gift granted to us through many.

...Let the persecuted Church give thanks in the midst of trials, and let that thanksgiving bear witness of your love to those who persecute them.

John 15:18-20

"If the world hates you, you know that it hated Me before it hated you...

I pray, Father, that you would give the persecuted Church a godly confidence in the midst of oppression. Let them be assured of your presence with them...

...If you were of the world, the world would love its own. Yet because you are not of the world, but I chose you out of the world, therefore the world hates you...

...Give the persecuted Church courage to face all adversity and understanding that their suffering is for the sake of your name. Let them stand with boldness to face all that they encounter...

...Remember the word that I said to you, 'A servant is not greater than his master.' If they persecuted Me, they will also persecute you. If they kept My word, they will keep yours also."

...Strengthen them in the knowledge that Jesus has suffered alongside them. I pray that their courage would be a witness of your strength and peace as they stand on the encouragement and comfort of your Word.

PRAY GOD'S WORD OVER
THE SEVEN SPHERES OF INFLUENCE:

1. Religion
   (The Church, Ministries, and Other Faiths)

2. Family and Marriages
   (Youth, Children, and the Sanctity of Marriage)

3. Education
   (All Schools, Universities, and Colleges)

4. Business
   (The Marketplace)

5. Government
   (Locally, Nationally, and Internationally)

6. Media
   (The Press, Television, Internet, and Social Networking)

7. Arts and Entertainment
   (Including Sports)

PRAY THE "FOUR CLAIMS" OVER
TODAY'S NATIONS

1. Claim... **Open Doors** (Colossians 4:2-3).
2. Claim... **Open Minds** (Acts 26:17b-18a).
3. Claim... **Open Hearts** (2 Corinthians 4:6).
4. Claim... **Open Heavens** (Isaiah 45:8).

Note: Visit www.EHC.org for real-time prayer requests from the front lines of world evangelism.

TODAY'S PROMISE FOR THE NATIONS

Isaiah 12:4-5 (NIV)

In that day you will say: "Give thanks to the LORD, proclaim his name; make known among the nations what he has done, and proclaim that his name is exalted...

Lord, I praise you in thanksgiving for all that you have done. I declare your greatness over these eight nations. I pray that they would know of your marvelous deeds and understand that your name is high above any other...

...Sing to the LORD, for he has done glorious things; let this be known to all the world."

...Let them lift their voices and worship you in song. Let the peoples sing of who you are and rejoice in your excellence.

TODAY'S NATIONS...

1.	Northern Marianas	(Pop. 50,000)	% of Christians: 13.34%
2.	Philippines	(Pop. 107,700,000)	% of Christians: 12.17%
3.	Taiwan	(Pop. 23,400,000)	% of Christians: 1.55%
4.	China	(Pop. 1,363,400,000)	% of Christians: 6.25%
5.	South Korea	(Pop. 49,000,000)	% of Christians: 16.43%
6.	North Korea	(Pop. 24,800,000)	% of Christians: 1.03%
7.	Japan	(Pop. 127,100,000)	% of Christians: 0.58%
8.	Mongolia	(Pop. 3,000,000)	% of Christians: 1.12%

Pray for the peace of Jerusalem—Psalm 122:6.

MY ADDITIONAL PERSONAL FOCUSES
(Include your own prayer list.)

_____

_____

_____

_____

_____

_____

_____

_____

_____

_____

_____

_____

_____

_____

_____

_____

_____

_____

_____

_____

25. DAY TWENTY-FIVE

TODAY'S WATCHMAN FOCUS:

THE MILITARY

(Those Serving in the Protection of the Nation)

Men and women who serve in the armed forces are willing to make the ultimate sacrifice, giving their lives to protect their nation and help maintain peace in the world. Pray for the various branches of the military in our nation and other nations as the Holy Spirit leads. Ask God to hold back any armies that may seek to create arbitrary conflicts that may lead to war in various regions of the world. Pray especially that Christians in all branches of service will "put on the whole armor of God" as described in Ephesians 6:10-20. Pray that godly officers and particularly chaplains will lead their troops with moral character and courage. Intercede for conflicts now underway in the nations that peace will be restored so that the Gospel can go freely throughout those nations or regions. Pray "by name" for servicemen and women you may know. Ask God to help you minister to the spiritual, emotional and practical needs of the spouses, children, and family members of military personnel who are away on dangerous deployments around the world.

DAY 25

TODAY'S PROMISE-PASSAGES

Psalm 33:12-20

Blessed *is* the nation whose God *is* the LORD, the people He has chosen as His own inheritance...

Father, today I lift my nation up to you. I pray that the people of my nation would choose you and your righteousness...

...The LORD looks from heaven; He sees all the sons of men. From the place of His dwelling He looks on all the inhabitants of the earth; He fashions their hearts individually; He considers all their works...

...As you look upon my nation and the nations across the earth, I bring before you those who are serving in the military. In some nations the military is a symbol of freedom, while in others it is a symbol of oppression. Whatever the case is in my nation, Lord, I pray by name for those I know who are in the military, as well as their families. Keep them safe and give them peace...

...No king *is* saved by the multitude of an army; a mighty man is not delivered by great strength. A horse *is* a vain hope for safety; neither shall it deliver *any* by its great strength...

I pray, Lord, that you would keep the hands of military leaders from unnecessary conflict and war. I ask that you would put freedom and security on the hearts of all levels of military personnel...

...Behold, the eye of the LORD *is* on those who fear Him, on those who hope in His mercy, to deliver their soul from death, and to keep them alive in famine...

...I pray against any kind of corruption in the military, Father. Purify the militaries of the nations where armed forces represent violence, restriction, corruption, or oppression...

...Our soul waits for the LORD; He *is* our help and our shield.

...And I pray that leaders and peoples of all nations would ultimately look to you as the source of security and hope.

Psalm 18:30-37

As for God, His way *is* perfect; the word of the LORD is proven; He *is* a shield to all who trust in Him...

I pray, Lord, for the men and women who serve in the military, especially those in my nation and those I know by name. I ask that you would protect them from all evil...

...For who *is* God, except the LORD? And who *is* a rock, except our God? *It is* God who arms me with strength, and makes my way perfect. He makes my feet like the *feet of* deer, and sets me on my high places...

...Keep them from fighting when they ought not to fight, and protect them from harm when they must. Preserve life and give leaders wisdom and discernment as they make policies and decisions...

...He teaches my hands to make war, so that my arms can bend a bow of bronze. You have also given me the shield of Your salvation; Your right hand has held me up, Your gentleness has made me great...

...I pray that Christian men and women who serve in militaries around the world would be strong witnesses for you, Father. Give them boldness to stand for what is right in all situations and to declare your salvation...

...You enlarged my path under me, so my feet did not slip. I have pursued my enemies and overtaken them; neither did I turn back again till they were destroyed.

...And I pray that you would make the righteous victorious, O Lord. Place your hand on all military affairs and direct them according to your will.

PRAY GOD'S WORD OVER THE SEVEN SPHERES OF INFLUENCE:

1. **Religion**
   (The Church, Ministries, and Other Faiths)

2. **Family and Marriages**
   (Youth, Children, and the Sanctity of Marriage)

3. **Education**
   (All Schools, Universities, and Colleges)

4. **Business**
   (The Marketplace)

5. **Government**
   (Locally, Nationally, and Internationally)

6. **Media**
   (The Press, Television, Internet, and Social Networking)

7. **Arts and Entertainment**
   (Including Sports)

PRAY THE "FOUR CLAIMS" OVER TODAY'S NATIONS

1. Claim... **Open Doors**   (Colossians 4:2-3).

2. Claim... **Open Minds**   (Acts 26:17b-18a).

3. Claim... **Open Hearts**   (2 Corinthians 4:6).

4. Claim... **Open Heavens**   (Isaiah 45:8).

Note: Visit www.EHC.org for real-time prayer requests from the front lines of world evangelism.

TODAY'S PROMISE FOR THE NATIONS

Psalm 9:10-11 (NIV)

Those who know your name will trust in you, for you, LORD, have never forsaken those who seek you...

You, O Lord, are faithful, never forsaking those who trust in you. I praise you for your steadfast love!

...Sing praises to the LORD, enthroned in Zion; proclaim among the nations what he has done.

I pray that the nations on my list today would worship you because you are God. Let them know of and experience this faithfulness and declare it to the world.

TODAY'S NATIONS...

1.	United States	(Pop. 318,900,000)	% of Christians: 26.43%
2.	Canada	(Pop. 34,800,000)	% of Christians: 7.70%
3.	Mexico	(Pop. 120,300,000)	% of Christians: 8.42%
4.	Guatemala	(Pop. 14,600,000)	% of Christians: 22.51%
5.	Belize	(Pop. 300,000)	% of Christians: 17.78%
6.	El Salvador	(Pop. 6,100,000)	% of Christians: 28.15%
7.	Honduras	(Pop. 8,500,000)	% of Christians: 22.07%

Pray for the peace of Jerusalem—Psalm 122:6.

MY ADDITIONAL PERSONAL FOCUSES
(Include your own prayer list.)

26. DAY TWENTY-SIX

TODAY'S WATCHMAN FOCUS:

HEALTH CARE

(Doctors, Nurses, and Medical Professionals)

One of the great needs in the nations concerns adequate health care. Sadly, many of the diseases in the world, especially in less-developed nations, are preventable or easily treated with proper medicines and hygiene. Pray today for those who do not have adequate medical care and for those who have a heart to help meet this need in our nation and the nations of the world. Ask God to use Christian doctors and nurses not only to minister to the physical needs of their patients but to the spiritual needs as well. Especially pray for those involved in medical missionary enterprises as they often risk contracting the very diseases they seek to treat. Pray "by name" for doctors, nurses and other medical professionals you may know. Pray that those who are followers of Christ in more blessed lands will make themselves available as frequently as possible to go on short-term mission trips to use their unique gifts to help the sick and suffering in less-developed nations of the world. In this way they will help fulfill God's promise of Psalm 72:12: "For he will deliver the needy who cry out, the afflicted who have no one to help" (NIV).

TODAY'S PROMISE-PASSAGES

Exodus 15:23-26

Now when they came to Marah, they could not drink the waters of Marah, for they *were* bitter. Therefore the name of it was called Marah. And the people complained against Moses, saying, "What shall we drink?"...

Father, we live in bodies hindered by the human condition in a world under the curse of sin. This means that millions of people suffer from all kinds of sicknesses and pains each day...

...So he cried out to the LORD, and the LORD showed him a tree. When he cast *it* into the waters, the waters were made sweet. There He made a statute and an ordinance for them, and there He tested them...

...But we thank you for providing care for our physical situation through health care professionals like doctors and nurses. Thank you for the insight into the human body you have given them and for the work they do...

...and said, "If you diligently heed the voice of the LORD your God and do what is right in His sight, give ear to His commandments and keep all His statutes, I will put none of the diseases on you which I have brought on the Egyptians. For I *am* the LORD who heals you."

...I praise you because you are ultimately our healer, and I pray that you would work through the hands of these medical professionals to mend brokenness and heal bodies all around the world. I pray by name for medical professionals I know and ask that you would guide their hands as they work to save lives.

Jeremiah 33:6-9

Behold, I will bring it health and healing; I will heal them and reveal to them the abundance of peace and truth...

Lord, I specifically lift up those who live in underdeveloped nations with limited access to health care. I pray for physical restoration to flow through these areas...

...And I will cause the captives of Judah and the captives of Israel to return, and will rebuild those places as at the first. I will cleanse them from all their iniquity by which they have sinned against Me, and I will pardon all their iniquities by which they have sinned and by which they have transgressed against Me...

...Thank you for medical professionals who spend time serving the people of foreign nations. I pray that you would protect them from the diseases and conditions they treat. Keep them healthy and allow them to remain focused on treating those who are sick and suffering. I also pray that you would train and send more of these who would care for your people...

...Then it shall be to Me a name of joy, a praise, and an honor before all nations of the earth, who shall hear all the good that I do to them; they shall fear and tremble for all the goodness and all the prosperity that I provide for it.

...And I pray that Christian medical professionals in all settings would have opportunity and boldness to share your love and your Gospel with those they see and treat. Let them bring spiritual healing as well as physical, and let them declare you as the true healer.

PRAY GOD'S WORD OVER THE SEVEN SPHERES OF INFLUENCE:

1. **Religion**
   (The Church, Ministries, and Other Faiths)

2. **Family and Marriages**
   (Youth, Children, and the Sanctity of Marriage)

3. **Education**
   (All Schools, Universities, and Colleges)

4. **Business**
   (The Marketplace)

5. **Government**
   (Locally, Nationally, and Internationally)

6. **Media**
   (The Press, Television, Internet, and Social Networking)

7. **Arts and Entertainment**
   (Including Sports)

PRAY THE "FOUR CLAIMS" OVER TODAY'S NATIONS

1. Claim... **Open Doors** (Colossians 4:2-3).
2. Claim... **Open Minds** (Acts 26:17b-18a).
3. Claim... **Open Hearts** (2 Corinthians 4:6).
4. Claim... **Open Heavens** (Isaiah 45:8).

Note: Visit www.EHC.org for real-time prayer requests from the front lines of world evangelism.

TODAY'S PROMISE FOR THE NATIONS

Isaiah 60:1-3 (NIV)

"Arise, shine, for your light has come, and the glory of the LORD rises upon you...

...See, darkness covers the earth and thick darkness is over the peoples, but the LORD rises upon you and his glory appears over you. Nations will come to your light, and kings to the brightness of your dawn."

O Lord, I pray that these seven nations would become shining lights of your glory. Let the people of these lands see and reflect the light of your name...

...I ask that each of these nations would find you in the midst of the darkness of the world. Let your glory fall upon them. And as these nations come to you, make their witness go forth into all the nations around them for the sake of the Gospel.

TODAY'S NATIONS...

1.	Nicaragua	(Pop. 5,800,000)	% of Christians: 26.87%
2.	Costa Rica	(Pop. 4,800,000)	% of Christians: 14.94%
3.	Panama	(Pop. 3,600,000)	% of Christians: 18.53%
4.	Curaçao	(Pop. 100,000)	% of Christians: 5.93%
5.	Jamaica	(Pop. 2,900,000)	% of Christians: 26.9%
6.	Cayman Islands	(Pop. 50,000)	% of Christians: 21.45%
7.	Bahamas	(Pop. 300,000)	% of Christians: 35.32%

Pray for the peace of Jerusalem—Psalm 122:6.

MY ADDITIONAL PERSONAL FOCUSES
(Include your own prayer list.)

_____
_____
_____
_____
_____
_____
_____
_____
_____
_____
_____
_____
_____
_____
_____
_____
_____

27. DAY TWENTY-SEVEN

TODAY'S WATCHMAN FOCUS:

THE ELDERLY

The elderly often face difficult challenges without complaint, and many have no one to help them in times of need. Pray that the younger generation will respect the unique gifts and wisdom of the elderly. Proverbs 16:31 says, "Gray hair is a crown of splendor; it is attained in the way of righteousness" (NIV). Ask God to reveal to elderly believers that they have a special opportunity to use their wisdom and spiritual maturity to be dedicated intercessors for the lost and others in need. Some may even feel called to be full-time intercessors. Pray that God will show them how to embrace this unique calling. Pray, too, about starting or joining an outreach team in your church or community that specifically provides assistance to the elderly. Pray "by name" for the elderly in your church who may need assistance. Befriend them, visiting them at home or in a senior care facility where they live. Pray for opportunities for sharing the Gospel with people who may have lived long lives but have not yet asked Jesus to come into their hearts.

TODAY'S PROMISE-PASSAGES

Psalm 37:23-31

The steps of a *good* man are ordered by the LORD, and He delights in his way. Though he fall, he shall not be utterly cast down; for the LORD upholds *him with* His hand...

Father, I praise you because all through our lives, you direct our steps and guide our ways. I thank you for elderly believers who have experienced your presence and grace in all situations in their lives...

...I have been young, and *now* am old; yet I have not seen the righteous forsaken, nor his descendants begging bread. He *is* ever merciful, and lends; and his descendants *are* blessed...

...I thank you for these precious ones who can reflect on long, full lives with you and recognize that your hand always upheld them and your mercies never failed...

...Depart from evil, and do good; and dwell forevermore. For the LORD loves justice, and does not forsake His saints; they are preserved forever, but the descendants of the wicked shall be cut off...

O Lord, I pray for an awareness among all generations of the value of the elderly in your family. I pray that younger generations would honor and respect those who have gone before them, cherishing the lessons learned and the memories shared...

...The righteous shall inherit the land, and dwell in it forever. The mouth of the righteous speaks wisdom, and his tongue talks of justice. The law of his God *is* in his heart; none of his steps shall slide.

...I pray by name for the elderly I know and love, that they would draw near to you and know your heart. I pray that you would continue to draw out the gifts you have placed in elderly believers, calling them to serve you with renewed passion.

Psalm 71:17-23

O God, You have taught me from my youth; and to this *day* I declare Your wondrous works...

Lord, I pray that the elderly who know you would never cease to praise your name and declare all that you have done...

...Now also when *I am* old and grayheaded, O God, do not forsake me, until I declare Your strength to *this* generation, Your power to everyone *who* is to come. Also Your righteousness, O God, *is* very high, You who have done great things; O God, who *is* like You?...

...I ask that you would make the elderly generation a witness to your greatness and faithfulness. Let them recognize your unfailing presence in their lives and declare it to all generations...

...*You,* who have shown me great and severe troubles, shall revive me again, and bring me up again from the depths of the earth. You shall increase my greatness, and comfort me on every side...

...I pray also, Father, for the elderly who may still have not received the salvation of your Son. Reveal yourself to them so that they might be restored to you and experience the joy of eternal life in Jesus...

...Also with the lute I will praise You— *and* Your faithfulness, O my God. To You I will sing with the harp, O Holy One of Israel. My lips shall greatly rejoice when I sing to You, and my soul, which You have redeemed.

...And I pray that all generations would take time to serve you by caring for and ministering to the elderly. Help younger generations be faithful to love as you love. I praise you, O Lord, because you are the Holy God who brings salvation to young and old alike.

PRAY GOD'S WORD OVER THE SEVEN SPHERES OF INFLUENCE:

1. **Religion**
   (The Church, Ministries, and Other Faiths)

2. **Family and Marriages**
   (Youth, Children, and the Sanctity of Marriage)

3. **Education**
   (All Schools, Universities, and Colleges)

4. **Business**
   (The Marketplace)

5. **Government**
   (Locally, Nationally, and Internationally)

6. **Media**
   (The Press, Television, Internet, and Social Networking)

7. **Arts and Entertainment**
   (Including Sports)

PRAY THE "FOUR CLAIMS" OVER TODAY'S NATIONS

1. Claim... **Open Doors**   (Colossians 4:2-3).
2. Claim... **Open Minds**   (Acts 26:17b-18a).
3. Claim... **Open Hearts**   (2 Corinthians 4:6).
4. Claim... **Open Heavens**   (Isaiah 45:8).

Note: Visit www.EHC.org for real-time prayer requests from the front lines of world evangelism.

TODAY'S PROMISE FOR THE NATIONS

Isaiah 14:26-27 (NLT)

"I have a plan for the whole earth, a hand of judgment upon all the nations...

...The LORD of Heaven's Armies has spoken—who can change his plans? When his hand is raised, who can stop him?"

O Lord, I lift up these seven nations to you and ask that you would pour out your redeeming love upon each of them...

...Stretch out your mighty hand toward them and let them see your glory, that they would worship you alone and declare your salvation among the nations!

TODAY'S NATIONS...

1.	Cuba	(Pop. 11,000,000)	% of Christians: 8.54%
2.	Haiti	(Pop. 10,000,000)	% of Christians: 15.98%
3.	Dominican Republic	(Pop. 10,300,000)	% of Christians: 9.36%
4.	Turks & Caicos Islands	(Pop. 50,000)	% of Christians: 32.20%
5.	Virgin Islands (U.K.)	(Pop. 30,000)	% of Christians: 28.95%
6.	Virgin Islands (U.S.)	(Pop. 100,000)	% of Christians: 24.36%
7.	Puerto Rico	(Pop. 3,600,000)	% of Christians: 26.86%

Pray for the peace of Jerusalem—Psalm 122:6.

MY ADDITIONAL PERSONAL FOCUSES
(Include your own prayer list.)

_____

_____

_____

_____

_____

_____

_____

_____

_____

_____

_____

_____

_____

_____

_____

_____

_____

_____

_____

_____

_____

_____

28. DAY TWENTY-EIGHT

TODAY'S WATCHMAN FOCUS:

THE HOMELESS

Today we place special emphasis during our prayer watch on those who lack a place to dwell, the homeless. In some regions of the world, vast numbers of children live and sleep in city slums, in culverts, and under bridges because that is their home. Even in more developed nations an increasing number of families are seeking help from local homeless shelters because they have no place to live. Many homeless, who often suffer from mental illness or addictions, sleep in parks and beside the road in bushes and shrubs. Pray for the well-being of the homeless and especially that the Church will rise up to help meet this growing need. Pray about ways that you and your church might become specifically involved in ministering to the homeless—providing food, clothing, and assistance in finding employment and meeting family needs. Especially remember ministries you know of devoted to this specific challenge. Above all, pray for opportunities for sharing the Gospel with homeless people who do not know the Lord. Encourage them with the words of the prophet Samuel: "The Lord...raises the poor from the dust and lifts the needy from the ash heap; he seats them with princes and has them inherit a throne of honor" (1 Samuel 2:7-8, NIV).

TODAY'S PROMISE-PASSAGES

Psalm 61:1-5

Hear my cry, O God; attend to my prayer. From the end of the earth I will cry to You, when my heart is overwhelmed; lead me to the rock that is higher than I...

Father, today I come to you on behalf of those in my nation and in nations around the world who are homeless. First of all, I pray that you would be the ultimate refuge of those who have no physical shelter. Hear their prayers and comfort them in your presence...

...For You have been a shelter for me, a strong tower from the enemy. I will abide in Your tabernacle forever; I will trust in the shelter of Your wings...

...I pray that those who have no home would lean on you to be their provider and refuge. Let them come to know you if they do not and learn to trust in you for all of their needs...

...For You, O God, have heard my vows; You have given *me* the heritage of those who fear Your name.

...And as they call on your name, O Lord, I pray that you would respond and demonstrate your concern for their physical well-being.

Deuteronomy 10:17-19

For the LORD your God *is* God of gods and Lord of lords, the great God, mighty and awesome, who shows no partiality nor takes a bribe...

I praise you, O Lord, for there is none like you in all the earth! You are the righteous God, powerful over all of creation.

...He administers justice for the fatherless and the widow, and loves the stranger, giving him food and clothing. Therefore love the stranger, for you were strangers in the land of Egypt.

As you have provided for us, Father, teach us to provide for others. Help us be like you as we reach out to the homeless and care for them as you lead. Give us opportunities to share the hope of your Gospel as we minister in practical ways.

Isaiah 16:3-5

"Take counsel, execute judgment; make your shadow like the night in the middle of the day; hide the outcasts, do not betray him who escapes...

I pray, Father, that your Church would stand up to defend the homeless and answer their cry for help. Let there be believers who will respond to your call to care for those who cannot care for themselves...

...Let My outcasts dwell with you, O Moab; be a shelter to them from the face of the spoiler. For the extortioner is at an end, devastation ceases, the oppressors are consumed out of the land...

...Make your Church a dwelling place for those who have no shelter. I pray that there would be ministries that would meet physical needs in practical ways while sharing the love of the Gospel...

...In mercy the throne will be established; and One will sit on it in truth, in the tabernacle of David, judging and seeking justice and hastening righteousness."

Extend your hand of provision through the Church, Father. Let the righteousness of your grace be established as your people care for the homeless in their own nation and in other nations.

Psalm 12:4-6

Who have said, "With our tongue we will prevail; our lips *are* our own; who *is* lord over us?"...

Father, I pray specifically for those who are homeless because they suffer from disabilities, addictions, or mental illness. I ask for healing and deliverance, O Lord...

... "For the oppression of the poor, for the sighing of the needy, now I will arise," says the LORD; "I will set *him* in the safety for which he yearns." The words of the LORD *are* pure words, *like* silver tried in a furnace of earth, purified seven times.

...And I pray that you would protect these of your children. Give them shelter and bring people to them who will act on their behalf in your name. Bring hope and light into such dark situations, Father, and let everyone involved see your mercy and your faithfulness.

PRAY GOD'S WORD OVER THE SEVEN SPHERES OF INFLUENCE:

1. Religion
   (The Church, Ministries, and Other Faiths)

2. Family and Marriages
   (Youth, Children, and the Sanctity of Marriage)

3. Education
   (All Schools, Universities, and Colleges)

4. Business
   (The Marketplace)

5. Government
   (Locally, Nationally, and Internationally)

6. Media
   (The Press, Television, Internet, and Social Networking)

7. Arts and Entertainment
   (Including Sports)

PRAY THE "FOUR CLAIMS" OVER TODAY'S NATIONS

1. Claim... **Open Doors**   (Colossians 4:2-3).
2. Claim... **Open Minds**   (Acts 26:17b-18a).
3. Claim... **Open Hearts**   (2 Corinthians 4:6).
4. Claim... **Open Heavens**   (Isaiah 45:8).

Note: Visit www.EHC.org for real-time prayer requests from the front lines of world evangelism.

TODAY'S PROMISE FOR THE NATIONS

Psalm 82:8 (NIV)

Rise up, O God, judge the earth, for all the nations are your inheritance.

O Lord, I pray that you would open doors for your righteousness to spread across the lands of these countries today. Let them worship you and be found holy and redeemed in your sight.

TODAY'S NATIONS...

#	Nation	Population	% of Christians
1.	Bermuda	(Pop. 70,000)	% of Christians: 24.17%
2.	Anguilla	(Pop. 20,000)	% of Christians: 17.22%
3.	Antigua & Barbuda	(Pop. 90,000)	% of Christians: 20.42%
4.	St. Kitts & Nevis	(Pop. 50,000)	% of Christians: 22.12%
5.	Montserrat	(Pop. 5,000)	% of Christians: 22.91%
6.	Guadeloupe	(Pop. 400,000)	% of Christians: 4.3%
7.	Dominica	(Pop. 70,000)	% of Christians: 15.77%
8.	Martinique	(Pop. 400,000)	% of Christians: 5.95%

Pray for the peace of Jerusalem—Psalm 122:6.

MY ADDITIONAL PERSONAL FOCUSES
(Include your own prayer list.)

29. DAY TWENTY-NINE

TODAY'S WATCHMAN FOCUS:

CRIME AND VIOLENCE

(Drug Cartels, Drug Trafficking, and Organized Crime)

Escalating crime and violence are symptoms of a society that has drifted away from God or outright rejected Him. Commenting on the end-times, Christ said: "Many false prophets will rise up and deceive many. And because lawlessness will abound, the love of many will grow cold. But he who endures to the end shall be saved" (Matthew 24:11-13). Pray against all those who would seek to tarnish our culture through criminal activity and all manner of corruption. Pray that God will show the younger generation that involvement with any kinds of "recreational" drug use does not only destroy their health, but fuels organized crime in the nations. Pray against the drug cartels of the world. In some nations, like Mexico, literally tens of thousands have died as the result of drug-related violence. Ask that God would cause the cartel leaders to make critical errors in how they conduct their business in such a way that leads to their downfall. Pray especially for the protection of Christian workers who work in the fearful atmosphere of these drug cartels. Pray also that those in law enforcement specifically focused on this problem will find more and better ways to combat this plague through modern technology and other means.

DAY 29

TODAY'S PROMISE-PASSAGES

Ephesians 4:17-24

This I say, therefore, and testify in the Lord, that you should no longer walk as the rest of the Gentiles walk, in the futility of their mind, having their understanding darkened, being alienated from the life of God, because of the ignorance that is in them, because of the blindness of their heart; who, being past feeling, have given themselves over to lewdness, to work all uncleanness with greediness...

...But you have not so learned Christ, if indeed you have heard Him and have been taught by Him, as the truth is in Jesus: that you put off, concerning your former conduct, the old man which grows corrupt according to the deceitful lusts...

...and be renewed in the spirit of your mind, and that you put on the new man which was created according to God, in true righteousness and holiness.

O Lord, I pray against crime and violence in my country and in countries all over the earth. I pray especially for nations that I know have higher crime rates and areas of the world that seem to be havens for criminals. I ask, Father, that you would rise up against such crime and violence. Make the plans of the wicked fail and frustrate the plots of the evil...

...Father, would you enlighten the darkened minds of criminals so that they would no longer desire such violence. Reveal your goodness and mercy to criminals so that they would instead seek to reflect your love...

...And protect your children from all corruption, Lord. Keep us holy and righteous so that we might become more like you as we seek your ways.

Psalm 11:2-7

For look! The wicked bend *their* bow, they make ready their arrow on the string, that they may shoot secretly at the upright in heart. If the foundations are destroyed, what can the righteous do?...

...The LORD *is* in His holy temple, the LORD's throne *is* in heaven; His eyes behold, His eyelids test the sons of men. The LORD tests the righteous, but the wicked and the one who loves violence His soul hates...

...Upon the wicked He will rain coals; fire and brimstone and a burning wind *shall be* the portion of their cup. For the LORD *is* righteous, He loves righteousness; His countenance beholds the upright.

Sometimes, Father, it can be easy to be overwhelmed by the crime and violence we witness in the world. The sinfulness of depraved humanity could cause us to live in fear of the world...

...But we know that you are Lord over all the earth. You are the righteous judge who sees all and will establish justice. You know all that man plans and does, and you hold the wicked accountable for their sin...

O Lord, let your holy people stand for your righteousness. Give us courage to speak of your ways and to stand against those who perpetrate violence and evil. Judge the wicked and uphold the cause of the upright.

2 Samuel 22:3-7

The God of my strength, in whom I will trust; my shield and the horn of my salvation, my stronghold and my refuge; my Savior, You save me from violence...

...I will call upon the LORD, *who is worthy* to be praised; so shall I be saved from my enemies. "When the waves of death surrounded me, the floods of ungodliness made me afraid. The sorrows of Sheol surrounded me; the snares of death confronted me...

...In my distress I called upon the LORD, and cried out to my God; He heard my voice from His temple, and my cry *entered* His ears..."

Father, I pray that you would be with the law enforcement of my nation and of other nations around the world as they fight crime and violence...

...I ask that law enforcement would be free of corruption so that officers can focus on administering justice. Give them strategies and resources, and make them effective in fighting all forms of crime and violence. Open their eyes to injustice and protect them from harm...

...You, O Lord, are righteous, and I pray that your righteousness would reign among the nations.

PRAY GOD'S WORD OVER THE SEVEN SPHERES OF INFLUENCE:

1. **Religion**
   (The Church, Ministries, and Other Faiths)

2. **Family and Marriages**
   (Youth, Children, and the Sanctity of Marriage)

3. **Education**
   (All Schools, Universities, and Colleges)

4. **Business**
   (The Marketplace)

5. **Government**
   (Locally, Nationally, and Internationally)

6. **Media**
   (The Press, Television, Internet, and Social Networking)

7. **Arts and Entertainment**
   (Including Sports)

PRAY THE "FOUR CLAIMS" OVER TODAY'S NATIONS

1. Claim... **Open Doors**   (Colossians 4:2-3).
2. Claim... **Open Minds**   (Acts 26:17b-18a).
3. Claim... **Open Hearts**   (2 Corinthians 4:6).
4. Claim... **Open Heavens**   (Isaiah 45:8).

Note: Visit www.EHC.org for real-time prayer requests from the front lines of world evangelism.

TODAY'S PROMISE FOR THE NATIONS

Isaiah 52:10 (NIV)

The LORD will lay bare his holy arm in the sight of all the nations, and all the ends of the earth will see the salvation of our God.

O Lord, I pray that you would reveal your holiness to these nations so that all of these peoples might experience your love and salvation!

TODAY'S NATIONS...

1. St. Lucia   (Pop. 200,000)   % of Christians: 14.46%

2. St. Vincent/Grenadines   (Pop. 100,000)   % of Christians: 36.73%

3. Barbados   (Pop. 300,000)   % of Christians:33.77%

4. Grenada   (Pop. 100,000)   % of Christians: 18.91%

5. Trinidad & Tobago   (Pop. 1,200,000)   % of Christians: 17.21%

6. Aruba   (Pop. 100,000)   % of Christians: 8.17%

7. French Guiana   (Pop. 200,000)   % of Christians: 5.46%

8. Suriname   (Pop. 600,000)   % of Christians: 12.41%

Pray for the peace of Jerusalem—Psalm 122:6.

MY ADDITIONAL PERSONAL FOCUSES
(Include your own prayer list.)

30. DAY THIRTY

TODAY'S WATCHMAN FOCUS:

THE ECONOMY

(Banks, Lending Institutions, and Greed)

The uncertainties of the economy affect all of us in different ways, including those ministries that seek to spread the Gospel globally. Very often missions organizations are the first to suffer in an economic slowdown. Pray for a healthy recovery in all sectors of the economy and that a spiritual awakening will take place that helps overcome the greed that caused so much of the recent economic woes. Pray also that if this is God's way of getting the attention of Christians to depend more on Him and to reject the ways of the world that a true revival will result. The great spiritual awakening of the 1850s, in which hundreds of thousands came to Christ, began as a result of a nationwide failure of America's banking system. In particular, as you serve as a watchman of the Lord today, ask God to allow Hebrews 13:5 to come alive in the hearts of His children: "Make sure that your character is free from the love of money, being content with what you have; for He Himself has said, 'I will never desert you, nor will I ever forsake you'" (paraphrase). More specifically, intercede for individuals you know of "by name" who have lost their jobs and are struggling financially as a result of a failing economy. Ask God to open opportunities for them to find meaningful employment. Additionally, pray that even amid these difficult times Christians will continue to give faithfully to their local churches and other worthy ministries. Pray also that those more blessed financially will be even more generous.

TODAY'S PROMISE-PASSAGES

Leviticus 26:3-12

"If you walk in My statutes and keep My commandments, and perform them, then I will give you rain in its season, the land shall yield its produce, and the trees of the field shall yield their fruit...

...Your threshing shall last till the time of vintage, and the vintage shall last till the time of sowing; you shall eat your bread to the full, and dwell in your land safely. I will give peace in the land, and you shall lie down, and none will make *you* afraid; I will rid the land of evil beasts, and the sword will not go through your land...

...You will chase your enemies, and they shall fall by the sword, before you. Five of you shall chase a hundred, and a hundred of you shall put ten thousand to flight; your enemies shall fall by the sword before you...

...For I will look on you favorably and make you fruitful, multiply you and confirm My covenant with you. You shall eat the old harvest, and clear out the old because of the new...

...I will set My tabernacle among you, and My soul shall not abhor you. I will walk among you and be your God, and you shall be My people."

Father, I thank you for the ways you have provided for me and for the resources you have entrusted to me. I pray that you would help me to be faithful with what you have given me.

Today I bring before you the issue of the economy, both in my nation and around the world. Recent years have been filled with economic strife, largely resulting from greed and corruption. I pray, Lord, that you would restore to my country and to the world a healthy, moral economy...

...I pray by name for churches and ministries I know that might be struggling because of the economy. As they serve you, sustain them financially so that they can continue their work...

...I pray also for people I know who have lost their jobs because of the economic downturn. Direct their paths as they search for new employment, and provide for their families in this season...

...And teach us to be entirely dependent on you for all of our needs. Let us see your hand in all these things and recognize that you are the true source and provider.

1 Timothy 6:5-10

Godliness is a *means of gain*. From such withdraw yourself. Now godliness with contentment is great gain...

O Lord, I understand that being obedient to you is not for the purpose of earning material wealth. Rather, as I become more like you, I learn to take joy in being content with the things you have already blessed me with...

...For we brought nothing into this world, and it is certain we carry nothing out. And having food and clothing, with these we shall be content...

...I am grateful for every need you meet—for every meal I eat and for every day I have clothes to wear. I pray that you would keep my heart from greed...

...But those who desire to be rich fall into temptation and a snare, and into many foolish and harmful lusts which drown men in destruction and perdition...

...Keep your children from the temptation of greed, Father. Let us value what you value and recognize every blessing we have from you...

...For the love of money is a root of all kinds of evil, for which some have strayed from the faith in their greediness, and pierced themselves through with many sorrows.

...Teach us to be content in all circumstances. Help us to be wise with the resources you have given us. And remind us to be generous as we give back to you through churches and ministries.

PRAY GOD'S WORD OVER THE SEVEN SPHERES OF INFLUENCE:

1. **Religion**
   (The Church, Ministries, and Other Faiths)

2. **Family and Marriages**
   (Youth, Children, and the Sanctity of Marriage)

3. **Education**
   (All Schools, Universities, and Colleges)

4. **Business**
   (The Marketplace)

5. **Government**
   (Locally, Nationally, and Internationally)

6. **Media**
   (The Press, Television, Internet, and Social Networking)

7. **Arts and Entertainment**
   (Including Sports)

PRAY THE "FOUR CLAIMS" OVER TODAY'S NATIONS

1. Claim... **Open Doors** (Colossians 4:2-3).
2. Claim... **Open Minds** (Acts 26:17b-18a).
3. Claim... **Open Hearts** (2 Corinthians 4:6).
4. Claim... **Open Heavens** (Isaiah 45:8).

Note: Visit www.EHC.org for real-time prayer requests from the front lines of world evangelism.

TODAY'S PROMISE FOR THE NATIONS

Isaiah 55:5 (NIV)

"Surely you will summon nations you know not, and nations that do not know you will hasten to you, because of the LORD your God, the Holy One of Israel, for he has endowed you with splendor."

O Lord, I pray that you would use your people to call each of these eight nations to you. Let them see your holiness through the witness of your children and glorify your name as they experience your salvation!

TODAY'S NATIONS...

1.	Guyana	(Pop. 700,000)	% of Christians: 13.87%
2.	Venezuela	(Pop. 28,900,000)	% of Christians: 10.62%
3.	Colombia	(Pop. 46,200,000)	% of Christians: 7.36%
4.	Ecuador	(Pop. 15,700,000)	% of Christians: 7.86%
5.	Peru	(Pop. 30,100,000)	% of Christians: 11.14%
6.	Brazil	(Pop. 202,700,000)	% of Christians: 25.01%
7.	French Polynesia	(Pop. 300,000)	% of Christians: 5.01%
8.	Chile	(Pop. 17,400,000)	% of Christians: 17.95%

Pray for the peace of Jerusalem—Psalm 122:6.

MY ADDITIONAL PERSONAL FOCUSES
(Include your own prayer list.)

_____

_____

_____

_____

_____

_____

_____

_____

_____

_____

_____

_____

_____

_____

_____

_____

_____

_____

_____

_____

31. DAY THIRTY-ONE

TODAY'S WATCHMAN FOCUS:

OUR NEIGHBORHOODS AND COMMUNITIES

Outside of our individual families and homes, the most immediate "sphere of influence" we have as followers of Christ for sharing the Good News is in our neighborhoods and communities. Establish a "prayer watch" for your neighborhood. Draw a map of your street and note the houses around yours, listing the names of each family. Periodically, even daily, walk throughout your neighborhood, praying for each family as you pass their houses. Pray that the Lord will give you spiritual insights into the needs of these neighbors so you can pray for them with understanding. Get to know your neighbors. When possible, engage them in a friendly conversation even if just to say "hello" and ask how they are doing. Then, prayerfully look for ways to share your own testimony with them. Pray, too, that Christ's Body locally and globally will reflect the joy and love of Christ so that people around them, in their particular neighborhoods and communities, will be drawn to Jesus. Pray about organizing a neighborhood Christ-sharing effort in your church. Look for ways to bless your neighbors through loving acts of kindness. Ask God to raise up a movement of "Lighthouses" of prayer and outreach that will shine the light of Christ's love in every neighborhood of our nation and beyond. As Jesus said, "Let your light so shine before men, that they may see your good works and glorify your Father in heaven" (Matthew 5:16).

TODAY'S PROMISE-PASSAGES

Jeremiah 29:4-7

Thus says the LORD of hosts, the God of Israel, to all who were carried away captive, whom I have caused to be carried away from Jerusalem to Babylon: Build houses and dwell *in them;* plant gardens and eat their fruit...

Father, I thank you for the neighborhood and community around me. Today, I bring the people of my community before you. I ask that you would make me a light of your love and a blessing to the people who live and work around me...

...Take wives and beget sons and daughters; and take wives for your sons and give your daughters to husbands, so that they may bear sons and daughters—that you may be increased there, and not diminished...

...I pray for each family and individual in my neighborhood. Make yourself known to them and let them receive your salvation. Call out more believers in my community to pray for your Gospel to go forth among the people here...

...And seek the peace of the city where I have caused you to be carried away captive, and pray to the LORD for it; for in its peace you will have peace.

...Give me insight as I pray for my neighborhood so that I might intercede specifically and with understanding. Guide me as I pray.

Matthew 5:14-16

"You are the light of the world. A city that is set on a hill cannot be hidden. Nor do they light a lamp and put it under a basket, but on a lampstand, and it gives light to all who are in the house...

Father, I pray for opportunities to share my testimony and the story of the Gospel with my neighbors and the members of my community. I pray for open hearts and minds and conversation that would be glorifying to you...

...Let your light so shine before men, that they may see your good works and glorify your Father in heaven."

...And let my words be a reflection of the things I do as I seek to serve you by serving the people who live around me.

Deuteronomy 28:1-8

"Now it shall come to pass, if you diligently obey the voice of the LORD your God, to observe carefully all His commandments which I command you today, that the LORD your God will set you high above all nations of the earth. And all these blessings shall come upon you and overtake you, because you obey the voice of the LORD your God...

..."Blessed *shall* you *be* in the city, and blessed *shall* you *be* in the country. Blessed *shall be* the fruit of your body, the produce of your ground and the increase of your herds, the increase of your cattle and the offspring of your flocks. Blessed *shall be* your basket and your kneading bowl...

..."Blessed *shall* you *be* when you come in, and blessed *shall* you *be* when you go out. The LORD will cause your enemies who rise against you to be defeated before your face; they shall come out against you one way and flee before you seven ways...

..."The LORD will command the blessing on you in your storehouses and in all to which you set your hand, and He will bless you in the land which the LORD your God is giving you."

O Lord, I pray that you would help me to be obedient to you in every way. Teach me to live according to your ways and to glorify you in everything I do. Make me an example of who you are to those who live and work around me. I want to be a light shining for you so that all those around me might see and come to you...

I ask, Father, for opportunities to bless and serve the community around me. Open my eyes to see needs that I might be able to meet and to practical ways I can bless the people who live here. Open doors for me to establish relationships so that I can share your love and kindness...

...Lord, I pray against anyone or anything that might harm my neighborhood or community. Protect the families and individuals who live here from the physical and spiritual attacks of the enemy. Let them find their security in you...

...Bless the land and the homes of my neighborhood, Father. Be the God of each person who lives here. Fill my community with joy and peace as the people here seek you.

PRAY GOD'S WORD OVER THE SEVEN SPHERES OF INFLUENCE:

1. Religion
   (The Church, Ministries, and Other Faiths)

2. Family and Marriages
   (Youth, Children, and the Sanctity of Marriage)

3. Education
   (All Schools, Universities, and Colleges)

4. Business
   (The Marketplace)

5. Government
   (Locally, Nationally, and Internationally)

6. Media
   (The Press, Television, Internet, and Social Networking)

7. Arts and Entertainment
   (Including Sports)

PRAY THE "FOUR CLAIMS" OVER TODAY'S NATIONS

1. Claim... **Open Doors** (Colossians 4:2-3).
2. Claim... **Open Minds** (Acts 26:17b-18a).
3. Claim... **Open Hearts** (2 Corinthians 4:6).
4. Claim... **Open Heavens** (Isaiah 45:8).

Note: Visit www.EHC.org for real-time prayer requests from the front lines of world evangelism.

TODAY'S PROMISE FOR THE NATIONS

Haggai 2:6-7 (NIV)

This is what the LORD Almighty says: "In a little while I will once more shake the heavens and the earth, the sea and the dry land. I will shake all nations, and the desired of all nations will come, and I will fill this house with glory," says the LORD Almighty.

Lord, I pray that you would shake these eight nations on my list today so that they might turn to you. Reveal your glory to them so that they would bow before you and worship you. Let your Gospel go forth as you awaken these nations.

TODAY'S NATIONS...

1.	Bolivia	(Pop. 10,600,000)	% of Christians: 16.13%
2.	Paraguay	(Pop. 6,700,000)	% of Christians: 6.82%
3.	Argentina	(Pop. 43,000,000)	% of Christians: 9.49%
4.	Uruguay	(Pop. 3,300,000)	% of Christians: 5.95%
5.	Falkland Islands	(Pop. 3,000)	% of Christians: 10.26%
6.	St. Pierre & Miquelon	(Pop. 6,000)	% of Christians: 0.34%
7.	Greenland	(Pop. 60,000)	% of Christians: 4.97%
8.	Iceland	(Pop. 300,000)	% of Christians: 3.94%

Pray for the peace of Jerusalem—Psalm 122:6.

MY ADDITIONAL PERSONAL FOCUSES
(Include your own prayer list.)

Spending a Meaningful Hour in Daily Prayer

(The Author's Testimony)

Nearly four decades ago I had a powerful prayer encounter that transformed my prayer life. Actually, it was an encounter that "gave" me my prayer life. In those days, just starting out in ministry, I prayed at times, but not consistently. I was what some might refer to as a "crisis pray-er." That's someone who prays when there is a crisis. I was not a consistent pray-er. I would have prayer times periodically and prayed during the week with my wife and other ministry staff, but I had no set time for devotional prayer on a regular basis.

One day I was in one of those crisis prayer modes, praying over pressing issues of the day, when God spoke to me in a profound way. During that time of prayer I had been listening to a cassette tape of a Christian leader (interestingly from another stream of Christ's Body far different from my denomination) as he described how God had called him years ago to devote at least one hour a day just to commune with His Son in secret prayer. He explained that he had not missed a day in 55 years. I was deeply humbled by his challenge as I realized I could not testify to that kind of consistency for even one week.

The leader then referred to Christ's encounter with His disciples in the Garden of Gethsemane the night before He went to the cross, as recorded in Matthew 26:36-41. It is here that we read of the intense struggle Christ faced as He prepared for the cross. At one point our Lord even pleads with His disciples: "My soul is overwhelmed with sorrow to the point of death. Stay here and keep watch with me" (Matthew 26:38, NIV).

Most students of the Bible know the rest of the story. When Christ goes further into the garden to engage in even more "warfare prayer," He suddenly returns to His disciples—no doubt desiring that they join Him in His battle. But the biblical narrative tells us that when Jesus returned to the group, He found them asleep. He then specifically chides Peter, "Could you not keep watch with me for one hour?" Jesus adds, "Watch and pray so that you will not fall into temptation. The spirit is willing, but the flesh is weak" (Matthew 26:41, NIV).

As I finished listening to the recorded challenge, I pondered these words repeatedly—"Could you not keep watch with me for one hour?" Soon I found myself weeping. Within moments I made a decision of a lifetime. With the Lord's help, I would not allow a day to go by for the rest of my life without having a set time of prayer for at least one hour. It was during the immediate days that followed that I read these words of a dynamic Christian leader of numerous generations past, Samuel Chadwick: "In these days there is no time to pray; but without time, and a lot of it, we shall never learn to pray. It ought to be possible to give God one hour out of twenty-four all to Himself." That sealed the deal! And now, some four decades later, I can testify that no decision, following my decision to give my life to Christ and serve Him in any way He chooses, has had a greater impact on my journey with Him.

Soon after this commitment was made, as I sought the Lord's wisdom on how I might sustain my daily set time of prayer, I was especially struck by the wording of Paul's challenge to Christians at Ephesus when he spoke of putting on the "whole armor" of the Lord as we engage in continuing spiritual warfare. After describing each aspect of the armor, Paul reminds these believers that the purpose of the armor is to fight and win our spiritual battles. He explains how:

"And pray in the Spirit on all occasions with all kinds of prayers and requests" (Ephesians 6:18, NIV). The Amplified Bible reads: "Pray at all times...with all [manner of] prayer and entreaty." This translation adds: "To that end keep alert and watch with strong purpose and perseverance, interceding in behalf of all the saints (God's consecrated people)."

As I pondered the phrase "all kinds of prayers and requests" (NIV) and "all manner of prayer and entreaty" (Amplified) I began thinking of various biblical aspects of prayer. It was from these early days of meditating on God's Word as it relates to prayer that the 12-step plan of prayer that follows was developed. The circle with this plan appears on page 216. Keep in mind that to spend just five minutes for each step will help you sustain an hour in prayer. It would be during your times of "watching," "intercession," and "petition" that appear on this list that you would include the daily focuses from this guide for each specific day of the month. You'll note we begin the 12 steps with praise and end with praise because praise is always appropriate to "seal" a prayer time. Do keep in mind this plan is merely a suggestion for those who desire to have a more complete time of prayer (as compared to just "asking" for things). Ask the Holy Spirit to help you keep your daily prayer watch fresh and meaningful. (For a fuller overview of these steps you may want to read my book, *The Hour That Changes the World*, Chosen Books.)

Remember to register your personal times of prayer (or local/area Walls of Prayer) at Every Home for Christ's...

GLOBAL WALL OF PRAYER

www.EHC.org

THE HOUR THAT CHANGES THE WORLD!

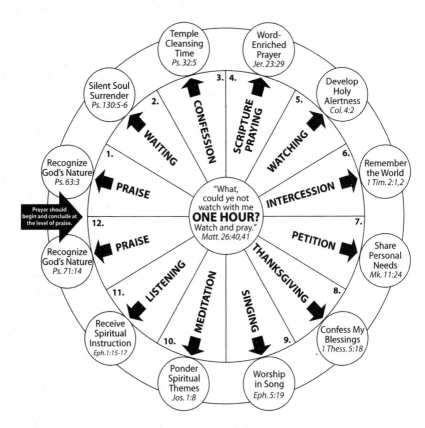

From *The Hour That Changes the World*, by Dick Eastman, Chosen Books, 2002. Used by permission of publisher.

"Oh! One hour with God infinitely exceeds all the pleasures and delights of the lower world."

—David Brainerd

PRAYING ONE HOUR IN FIVE-MINUTE SEGMENTS

1. Praise:
A time of *exaltation*

Scripture: Psalm 63:3
"Because your loving kindness is better than life,
my lips shall praise You."

2. Waiting:
A time of *anticipation*

Scripture: Psalm 130:5-6
"I wait for the LORD...my soul waits for the Lord more
than those who watch for the morning."

3. Confession:
A time of *examination*

Scripture: Psalm 32:5
"I acknowledged my sin...I will confess my transgressions."

4. Scripture Praying:
A time of *appropriation*

Scripture: Jeremiah 23:29
"Is not my Word like a fire?...and like a hammer
that breaks the rock in pieces?"

5. Watching:
A time of *observation*

Scripture: Colossians 4:2
"Continue earnestly in prayer, being vigilant
in it with thanksgiving."

6. Intercession:
A time of *intervention*

Scripture: 1 Timothy 2:1-2
"...I exhort first of all that supplications, prayers, intercessions,
and giving of thanks be made for all men, for kings and all
who are in authority, that we may lead a quiet and
peaceable life in all godliness and reverence."

7. Petition:
A time of *expectation*

Scripture: Mark 11:24
"Therefore I say to you, whatever things you ask when you pray,
believe that you receive *them*, and you will have *them*."

8. Thanksgiving:
A time of *appreciation*

Scripture: 1 Thessalonians 5:18
"In everything give thanks; for this is the will of
God in Christ Jesus for you."

9. Singing:
A time of *edification*

Scripture: Ephesians 5:19
"Speaking to one another in psalms and hymns
and spiritual songs, singing and making
melody in your heart to the Lord."

10. Meditation:
A time of *evaluation*

Scripture: Joshua 1:8
"This Book of the Law shall not depart from your mouth, but you
shall meditate in it day and night, that you may observe to do
according to all that is written in it. For then you will make your
way prosperous, and then you will have good success."

11. Listening:
A time of *revelation*

Scripture: Ephesians 1:15-17
"Therefore, I...do not cease to give thanks for you, making
mention of you in my prayers: that the God...may give
to you the spirit of wisdom and revelation..."

12. Praise:
A time of *jubilation*

Scripture: Psalm 71:14
"...I will hope continually, and will praise You yet more and more."

In-Depth "Online" Studies Taught by Dick Eastman

(Note: Student worksheets from each lesson can be downloaded and printed in black and white or in color.)

The Change the World School of Prayer...

...Featuring seven dynamic lessons, each divided into three sessions of approximately 30 minutes per session. Learn how to tap into the power of prayer, how to pray systematically for the nations and how to hear God's voice when you pray. Experience prayer insights that have now impacted more than three million believers worldwide who have studied these practical principles of praying with purpose and power. Also available as a part of this course is a 75-page students' workbook and Dick Eastman's 350-page book also titled *The Change the World School of Prayer.*

VISIT EHC'S WEBSITE FOR THE ONLINE COURSE AND FOR MORE INFORMATION ON "THE SCHOOL OF PRAYER."

www.EHC.org

(Not available outside the U.S.)

Also Available Online...

The University of the Word
Taught by Dick Eastman

A multi-hour course featuring 12 principles of mature Christian living founded in God's Word. Through these principles the student will learn how to live, learn, and love God's Word daily. The 12 main lessons are divided into two parts of approximately 35 minutes each. The full course includes insights into how one can mark and cross-reference his or her Bible in a daily, joyful way. (visit www.EHC.org.)

Visit **www.EHC.org** for other resources by Dick Eastman including his numerous books on prayer and evangelism and Every Home for Christ's free color World Prayer Map (also available in a children's version). **(Not available outside the U.S.)**

Your Invitation to Visit the "Watchman Wall" at The Jericho Center for Global Evangelism

The Jericho Center for Global Evangelism in Colorado Springs, Colorado, USA, is the international headquarters of Every Home for Christ (EHC), a ministry serving the global Body of Christ in taking the Good News of Jesus Christ to every home on earth. The Jericho Center also houses an 8,000 square-foot area dedicated to mobilizing and training strategic, worship-saturated prayer for harvest advances throughout the world. Included in this area is a 400-seat Watchman Training Center, as well as a unique "prayer wall" patterned after the ancient Wailing Wall in Jerusalem. This wall is constructed with 50 tons of actual Jerusalem stone from a quarry where stone came from for the original Western Wall.

Serving as a visual symbol of "Watchmen on the Wall" (see Isaiah 62:6-7) who pray day and night without ceasing, this unique Wall also serves as a headquarters for mobilizing continual prayer for all the nations of the world, recruiting believers globally to find their place on a "Wall of Prayer" in their area. The ultimate goal of the Watchman Training Center is to fill every moment of every day—in every time zone and major city of the world—with focused intercession and worship for global awakening. To assist in spreading this vision to the nations is a new student volunteer mission movement called "The Prayer Corps," involving mature young adults trained at and sent out from the Watchman Training Center.

Additionally, EHC's on-site "Wall of Prayer" includes 13 individual "prayer grottos" (rooms) for intercessors who wish to spend whole or half days in intensive intercession for the nations. Twelve of these rooms are named after the tribes of Israel, and the remaining grotto is called "The Back to Jerusalem Room" to highlight the Chinese Church's vision to someday send tens of thousands of Christian missionaries along the old silk roads through Central Asia and the Middle East—all the way back to Jerusalem. You are invited to visit The Jericho Center in Colorado Springs, Colorado, and spend time in a prayer grotto or bring a small group for a season of prayer in our "harp and bowl" (Revelation 5:8-10) prayer room. Please call or email in advance to reserve a room. (**visit www.EHC. org.**)

Every Home for Christ's Vision

Every Home for Christ exists to serve the Church
to reach every home on earth with the Gospel.

Every Home for Christ's
Three Unalterable Convictions

1. The Great Commission must be taken literally.
"All the world" and "every creature." *(Mark 16:15)*

2. Without unity, finishing the task of world evangelization
is impossible. *(John 17:21-23)*

3. Prayer, alone, will remove every obstacle that
stands in the way of fulfilling the
Great Commission. *(Mark 11:22-23)*

EHC's History at a Glance

The ministry of Every Home for Christ began in Canada in 1946.

The first Every Home Campaign (EHC) involving systematic
home-by-home evangelism began in Japan in 1953.

There are currently EHC campaigns in more than 130 nations.

More than 3.5 billion gospel booklets and face-to-face contacts have
been made. To date more than 139 million decision cards
and responses have been followed-up.

Decisions/responses are followed-up with Bible lessons. Where there
are no churches, Christ Group fellowships are planted. To date,
more than 245,000 Christ Groups have been formed.

In a recent 12-month period EHC workers visited an average
of 252,000 families every day, with an average of 44,000
decisions/responses received daily.

More than 30,000 workers worldwide are involved with EHC
in any given month, of which 90 percent are volunteers.